The Government Manager's Guide to Contract Negotiation

The Government Manager's Essential Library

1. *The Government Manager's Guide to Appropriations Law*, William G. Arnold, CDFM-A
2. *The Government Manager's Guide to Source Selection*, Charles D. Solloway, Jr., CPCM
3. *The Government Manager's Guide to Contract Negotiation*, LeGette McIntyre
4. *The Government Manager's Guide to Plain Language*, Judith Gillespie Myers, Ph.D.
5. *The Government Manager's Guide to the Work Breakdown Structure*, Gregory T. Haugan, Ph.D., PMP
6. *The Government Manager's Guide to Strategic Planning*, Kathleen E. Monahan
7. *The Government Manager's Guide to Project Management*, Jonathan Weinstein, PMP and Timothy Jaques, PMP
8. *The Government Manager's Guide to Leading Teams*, Lisa DiTullio
9. *The Government Manager's Guide to Earned Value Management*, Charles I. Budd, PMP, and Charlene S. Budd, Ph.D., CPA, CMA, CFM, PMP
10. *The Government Manager's Guide to the Statement of Work*, Michael G. Martin, PMP
11. *The Government Manager's Guide to Contract Law*, Terrence O'Connor

The Government Manager's Guide to Contract Negotiation

LeGette McIntyre

MANAGEMENTCONCEPTS PRESS

MANAGEMENTCONCEPTS PRESS
8230 Leesburg Pike, Suite 800
Tysons Corner, VA 22182
(703) 790-9595
Fax: (703) 790-1371
www.managementconcepts.com

Copyright © 2013 by Management Concepts, Inc.

All rights reserved. No part of this book may be reproduced or utilized in any form or by any means, electronic or mechanical, including photocopying, recording, or by an information storage and retrieval system, without permission in writing from the author and the publisher, except for brief quotations in review articles.

Library of Congress Control Number: 2013933786

ISBN 978-1-56726-412-8

Printed in the United States of America

Portions of this book have been adapted with permission from *Essentials for Government Contract Negotiators* by LeGette McIntyre, © 2006 by Management Concepts, Inc. All rights reserved.

ABOUT THE AUTHOR

LeGette (LeGs) McIntyre is President of McIntyre, Inc., a Florida-based corporation specializing in all areas of federal acquisition support and training. He has 20 years of experience as an Air Force leader and over 30 years of experience in the federal acquisition process. He has extensive experience in contract negotiations, as well as in applying acquisition principles, business process analysis, strategic planning, corporate staffing and organizational analysis capture, and market research techniques to all facets of the procurement process. He is known as one of the premiere acquisition instructors throughout the government and is a nationally recognized speaker on acquisition and contracting issues. He has a BS in business administration from The Citadel and an MBA from the University of Missouri. He currently resides in Niceville, Florida, where he pursues his passion for sailing.

LeGs and his associates offer one, two, and three-day seminars based on the negotiation principles discussed in this book and his more detailed book, *Essentials for Government Contract Negotiators*. For information or to register, e-mail or call LeGs at legsmcintyre@aol.com, (850) 499-1404.

To my wonderful son, Christopher. For all of his nine years, he has put up with his Daddy's frequent work trips away from home without complaint. He reminds his mother Jill and me that it's important to laugh, relax, have fun, and not take ourselves too seriously. He is pure joy God has inserted into our lives. For nine years old, he's also one heck of a good negotiator!

CONTENTS

PREFACE xv

ACKNOWLEDGMENTS xvii

CHAPTER 1: Government Negotiation Goals 1
    Best Value 2
    Performance-Based Contracting 2

CHAPTER 2: The Negotiation Team 5
    Characteristics of a Negotiation Team 5
    Team Members 6
    Briefing the Team 6

CHAPTER 3: Gathering Data and Establishing Prenegotiation Objectives 7
    Gathering Data 7
    Establishing Prenegotiation Objectives 8

CHAPTER 4: Researching the Other Party 11
    Researching the Company 11
    Researching the Company's Negotiators 12
    Information Sources 13
    Info-Gathering Tips 14

CHAPTER 5: Developing the Negotiation Plan 17
    Overall Objectives 17
    Background Information 17
    Team Members 18
    Negotiation Objectives 18
    Major Issues 19
    Negotiation Strategy 19
    Schedule and Logistics 22

CHAPTER 6: Developing the Negotiation Agenda 25

CHAPTER 7: Assigning Negotiation Roles 27
    Team Leader 27
    Good Cop 28
    Bad Cop 28
    Technocrat 29
    Sweeper 30

CHAPTER 8: Using Tactics in Negotiations 31

CHAPTER 9: Time Tactics 33
    The Time Pressure Tactic 33
    Counters to the Time Pressure Tactic 34
    The Time Investment Tactic 35
    Counters to the Time Investment Tactic 35

CHAPTER 10: Question and Trial Balloon Tactics 37
    The Question Tactic 37
    The Trial Balloon Tactic 39
    Counters to Question and Trial Balloon Tactics 39

CHAPTER 11: The Silence Tactic 41
    Counters to the Silence Tactic 42

CHAPTER 12: The Vise Tactic 43
    Counters to the Vise Tactic 43

CHAPTER 13: The Order-of-Issues Tactic 45
    Counters to the Order-of-Issues Tactic 46

CHAPTER 14: The Good Cop/Bad Cop Tactic 47
    Counters to the Good Cop/Bad Cop Tactic 48

CHAPTER 15: The Caucus Tactic 49
    Counters to the Caucus Tactic 50

CHAPTER 16: The Nibble Tactic 51
    Counters to the Nibble Tactic 52

CHAPTER 17: The Ambiguous Authority Tactic 53
    Counters to the Ambiguous Authority Tactic 54

CHAPTER 18: The Bracketing Tactic 55
    Counters to the Bracketing Tactic 56

CHAPTER 19: The Set-Aside Tactic 57
    Counters to the Set-Aside Tactic 57

CHAPTER 20: The Tradeoff Tactic 59
    Counters to the Tradeoff Tactic 60

CHAPTER 21: The Coupling Tactic 61
    Counters to the Coupling Tactic 61

CHAPTER 22: The Empty Pockets Tactic 63
    Countering the Empty Pockets Tactics 64

CHAPTER 23: The Climate Control Tactic 65
    Counters to the Climate Control Tactic 65

CHAPTER 24: The Strength-in-Numbers Tactic 67
    Counters to the Strength-in-Numbers Tactic 67

CHAPTER 25: The Walk-in-the-Woods Tactic 69
    Counters to the Walk-in-the-Woods Tactic 70

CHAPTER 26: The Anger Tactic 71
    Handling Anger 71

CHAPTER 27: The Personal Attack Tactic 73
    Handling Personal Attacks 73

CHAPTER 28: The Guilt-Trip Tactic 75
    Countering the Guilt-Trip Tactic 75

CHAPTER 29: The Frustration Tactic ... 77
Handling Frustration ... 77

CHAPTER 30: The Walkout Tactic ... 79
Counters to the Walkout Tactic ... 79

CHAPTER 31: The Lock-In Tactic ... 81
The Classic Lock-In Tactic ... 81
The Fait Accompli ... 81
Take It or Leave it ... 82
Counters to the Lock-In Tactic ... 82

CHAPTER 32: The Decoy Tactic ... 85
Counters to the Decoy Tactic ... 85

CHAPTER 33: The Deliberate Mistake Tactic ... 87
Phony Facts ... 87
Countering Phony Facts ... 88
Deliberate Omissions and Errors ... 90
Countering Deliberate Omissions and Errors ... 90

CHAPTER 34: Setting the Stage for the Negotiation ... 91
Reserve the Rooms ... 92
Clear Schedules ... 92
Check Availability of Your Extended Negotiation Team and Supporting Cast ... 93
Set Up the Room ... 93
Plan Lunch and Breaks ... 95

CHAPTER 35: Opening the Negotiation ... 97
Make Introductions ... 97
Establish Your Authority ... 98
Verify the Other Side's Authority ... 98
Make an Opening Statement ... 99

    Allow the Other Side to Make an Opening Statement 99

    Transition into your First Tactic 100

    Listen! 100

CHAPTER 36: Conducting the Negotiation 103

    Do's 103

    Don'ts 105

CHAPTER 37: Closing the Negotiation 107

    Preparing to Close 107

    Ways to Close 108

    Ensuring Total Agreement 110

    Making Everyone Feel Like a Winner 111

CHAPTER 38: Documenting the Negotiation 113

    The Price Negotiation Memorandum 114

    Obtaining a Release of Claims 114

    Obtaining Required Reviews and Approvals 115

    Documenting Postaward Actions and Providing
        Postaward Notifications 115

    Preparing the Contract, Award, or Agreement Document 115

CHAPTER 39: Final Thoughts 117

REFERENCES AND RESOURCES 119

INDEX 121

PREFACE

This book is a logical outgrowth of and follow-on to my first book about negotiation, *Essentials for Government Contract Negotiators*, which was published in 2006. That book addressed the need for true, focused, effective training for folks on the government side of the negotiation table. It actually started as a script for a two-day negotiation seminar, but soon it ballooned into the manuscript for a 400-page book. There was that much I thought I needed to cover about contract negotiation.

I am truly blessed that that book has been a Management Concepts bestseller since it was published. And, of course, I think everyone who negotiates should own at least one copy of it! However, it's a pretty thick, all-encompassing book—even delving into the psychology behind certain strategies and tactics. In the back of my mind, I had always toyed with the idea of creating a smaller, scaled-down, "just the essential facts" version of my tome. Coincidentally my publisher had been thinking along these same lines.

My publisher approached me and said it was launching a new series of books that would have the title *The Government Manager's Guide to* _____, filling in the blank with various essential areas important for government professionals to master. These books would serve essentially as quick reference guides for the working professional, rather than bedside table reading material or bookshelf reference space fillers. They were going to be designed to be easy to follow, concise, and quickly useful. Wow, just what I had been thinking! Management Concepts Press wanted the subject of contract negotiation to be one of the books in the new series. I quickly agreed, and the result is this book.

This book will benefit anyone who is involved in any way as a government negotiator across all federal agencies: contracting officers, specialists, administrators, price analysts, cost analysts, legal staff, small business specialists, program personnel, program managers, project managers, and contracting officer representatives. While it is geared to federal government negotiators, state and local contract negotiators, as well as contractors, will also find this book useful. Finally, since most negotiation principles, strategies, and tactics are universal, this book will be helpful to anyone needing to apply sound negotiation strategies and tactics in their personal life. It will help you understand the negotiation process, plan for it, develop strategies and tactics, anticipate and counter the other side's strategies and tactics, and conclude and document the negotiation. Knowing the strategies and tactics in this book will help you the next time you buy a car, a house, or a used table at a flea market. My hope is that this book will become extremely dog-eared from use!

—LeGs McIntyre

ACKNOWLEDGMENTS

When I sat down to write my first negotiation book, I figured I could knock it out rather quickly and effortlessly. After all, I was an expert on negotiation, wasn't I? Boy, was I in for a rude awakening! I found out that knowing stuff and writing about stuff are two completely different ballgames. Although I did much writing after hours while I was on the road training, I still had to take huge chunks out of what was supposed to be family time to complete that book. This included a month-long marathon writing sprint at the end, when I seldom could do anything with the ones I loved the most. They were generally forgiving about my absences, but my wife Jill made me promise to never, never, never write another book—ever again. Ever. Then my publisher, Myra Strauss, approached me with the suggestion for *this* book and sold me on writing one more time.

I certainly owe Myra and the entire publishing team at Management Concepts Press a big "thanks" for talking me into writing this book. But I must reserve my biggest expression of gratitude to my family, who at first reluctantly relented and then fully supported me in this endeavor. Thanks to my sons Myles and Christopher, and my daughter Shelby. Special thanks go out, of course, to my beautiful wife Jill. She's the one who gave me ultimate "permission" to write this book, fully knowing what it would entail. How anybody can succeed at anything without a loving and supporting family in their corner amazes me.

Chapter 1

GOVERNMENT NEGOTIATION GOALS

The government can't even come close to providing all the goods and services it needs to operate using in-house resources, so it has long been policy to meet its requirements for supplies and services from the commercial marketplace. Taxpayers expect the government to do this in a smart manner, at fair and reasonable prices—hence the need for trained government negotiators. The job of a government negotiator is to satisfy the government customer's needs in terms of cost, timeliness, and quality—while upholding the highest ethical standards at all times. As a government negotiator, you must also comply with all laws and regulations concerning socioeconomic policy, reporting and accounting requirements, transparency, and the like. No government negotiator should start planning for a negotiation without first considering and thoroughly understanding these basic goals.

Hand in hand with the concept of fairness is the requirement to negotiate in good faith. Negotiating in good faith means that you must honestly strive to reach agreement on differences through compromise and not take unfair advantage of the other party. Leading a contractor on in a negotiation by implying that you have funds available to consummate the deal when in fact you know you don't is an example of negotiating in bad faith. In this case, at the very least, you have caused the contractor to expend time, energy, effort, and money to no good purpose. This is simply not fair to the contractor.

Your ultimate goal—the result of your negotiation—should be to reach an agreement that is fair and reasonable to both parties. But be cautious! Your counterparts in industry do not share the same requirements to comply with laws that you are bound to as a government negotiator. Nor do they share the goal of being fair and reasonable to you.

> **Manager Alert**
> Because you represent the government, you are held to a higher standard than those you negotiate with. You must be fair and reasonable to both sides.

BEST VALUE

The ultimate goal of every government acquisition is best value. Achieving best value is simply selecting a contractor based on the overall benefit—the best value—to the government considering price and other factors. Although it's true that sometimes price alone is the best determinant of best value, other factors, such as past performance, are often considered.

We can look at each contractor's technical approach to solving our problem, as well as many non-price factors such as resumes of key personnel, to help us pick the "right" contractor. We simply have to state those evaluation factors when we go out with our solicitation. When the proposals come in, we can "trade off" technical superiority against price. In other words, we can award to a contractor other than the low-priced contractor on the basis of the technical superiority of that company's solution—provided we can justify spending the extra bucks to get the extra bang.

That's great news for our customers, but it complicates your job as a contracting officer and a negotiator. No longer is price the only factor to be negotiated. Rarely will the contractor's idea of best value—the mix of price and technical factors submitted with the proposal—be your idea of best value. The mix often has to be negotiated, and this can get complicated. You must negotiate not just price, but also factors such as warranty terms, level of effort, delivery dates, level of government involvement and the validity and chance of success of various technical approaches. And you ultimately have to balance all these factors against price.

PERFORMANCE-BASED CONTRACTING

Government negotiators also have the goal of being as performance-based as possible in all aspects of the acquisition. Instead of dictating the specifications—the process for solving our problem—to contractors, we now simply state what we need in terms of outputs and invite *them* to come up with the process. That's performance-based contracting. Although this approach often ensures that our needs are better satisfied, it also greatly increases the difficulty you'll face in proposal analysis and ultimately in negotiations. When the proposals come in, you can no longer do an apples-to-apples comparison, because all the proposed technical solutions can be vastly different—and they come with different price tags.

> **Manager Alert**
> If you are vaguely dissatisfied with a contractor's performance but can't point to anything specific in the contract that they are violating, that's a sure sign your contract is not written as performance-based as it should be.

One company, for instance, may propose to satisfy our need by relying heavily on manual labor, while another contractor proposes to rely heavily on automation and technology. Both proposals can meet our needs; they just reflect different ways of getting to the result. Because the proposals can be substantially different, you have to develop separate negotiation plans for each contractor tailored to the strengths and weaknesses unique to each proposal. When you negotiate with these contractors, you will have to talk about the merits of their particular technical approaches in addition to negotiating price.

To complicate matters, you start off with an immediate negotiation disadvantage. The contractors are the experts in their particular technical approaches, not you. After all, they wrote it; you just reviewed it. They are in a superior knowledge position about the process because they came up with the process—and the process will drive the price. Only through careful planning and good negotiation skills can you overcome this inherent disadvantage and ensure that the government ends up with a fair and reasonable deal.

Chapter 2

THE NEGOTIATION TEAM

The contracting officer, usually the lead negotiator, is responsible for putting the government negotiation team together: sizing it, choosing the team members, and training them. Who are your potential team players, and how do you pull this team together?

CHARACTERISTICS OF A NEGOTIATION TEAM

A negotiation team is truly a unique creation. Generally, you'll have a different team for each negotiation, depending on the customer you are supporting and the technical knowledge required for whatever you are buying. This allows you to tailor the team composition and size to fit the situation. Consider the overall scope of the negotiation, expertise required, complexity, dollar value, visibility, and the like when creating the team.

Be aware that the team will not be a naturally cohesive unit. Members will be drawn from different functions; they know they'll be together as a team for a short time and will then go back to their "normal" jobs. Your challenge will be to lead this disjointed collection of individuals through a successful negotiation, and that will take patience, training, and tact. Try to fit the right people in the right places for the negotiation. This will enable you to focus on leading the team and concentrating your talents on the overall outcome of the negotiation.

> **Manager Alert**
> Successfully leading a negotiating team is a challenge. Usually the team members don't work for you; they are dedicated to your effort only part time, and they are distracted by their "real" jobs.

TEAM MEMBERS

You are responsible for selecting the team, so bring in folks who represent the particular expertise you'll need for that negotiation. Some of the traditional team members you could include are as follows:
- Team leader
- Contract specialists
- Price analysts/cost analysts
- Technical representatives/technical experts
- Program managers
- Auditors, attorneys, small business specialists, property specialists, etc., as needed.

BRIEFING THE TEAM

Schedule a team meeting with all participants as soon as possible. Use this forum to establish your authority as the team leader, introduce members to each other, and assign and clarify each team member's role. Attach action dates to any duties you assign, making sure to reserve some duties for yourself so your team can see that you are participating and not just delegating. Make sure to assign someone the task of taking minutes of the meeting.

End the kickoff meeting by highlighting the importance of the negotiation to the customer and taxpayers, and stress preparation as the key to success. Encourage all team members to make the negotiation effort their #1 priority. Provide the team members—and their upper management—a copy of the meeting minutes as soon as possible. (Make sure the minutes have appropriate markings if they contain source selection or proprietary information.)

Chapter 3

GATHERING DATA AND ESTABLISHING PRENEGOTIATION OBJECTIVES

The key next steps are gathering data and establishing prenegotiation objectives.

GATHERING DATA

A wealth of information that can help you and your team prepare for the negotiation is available. Remember the main reason you are gathering data: to verify that the contractor's proposed pricing, terms, and conditions are fair and reasonable and, if they are not, to develop and defend *your* position on what you consider fair and reasonable. Keeping this in mind will help you limit your search and prevent information overload.

Bear in mind that the data-gathering you're doing at this stage is solely to help you come up with your positions, given the contractor's proposal and your customer's needs. (Later you will gather additional data to give you important clues and insights into the folks who will be sitting across the table from you.) The most important sources of data to help you establish your negotiation positions include the following:

- Requirements package e.g., statement of objectives, statement of work, performance work statement
- Solicitation document (request for quotes, request for proposals, etc.)
- Contractor's proposal

- Technical evaluation report
- Fact-finding/exchanges
- Price analysis and cost analysis
- Acquisition histories.

Assign responsibility for gathering and analyzing the data to individual team members during the kickoff meeting. Tailor the amount and kinds of data you'll gather to the size and complexity of your particular situation to avoid "analysis paralysis." If you try to collect *all* available information before you negotiate, you'll never negotiate—you'll spend all your time collecting data. Collect enough to make smart decisions and press on!

ESTABLISHING PRENEGOTIATION OBJECTIVES

Once you have gathered the relevant data, the next step is to establish your prenegotiation objectives. To do this, you first need to use what you have learned in data-gathering to establish your priorities for the negotiation. Knowing your priorities is essential to establishing your negotiation plan; they will serve as a guide and focal point when your plan encounters the confusion and shifting positions that will inevitably arise during a negotiation.

> **Manager Alert**
> You must know your priorities—and their order of importance—to develop an effective negotiation plan.

In reality, some of your priorities may already be dictated to you. Other priorities may be constrained by time, money, contract type, law, and policies. Your own experience and your team members' experience (or lack of experience) may also constrain what you can focus on as priorities. But there are usually many issues over which you and your team have a fair amount of control. What's important to you—and where the issues rank in importance to each other—will affect how you plan your negotiation.

Your customers should have the lead role in identifying priorities for the negotiation. Only they can tell you how high factors such as quality, timeliness (the schedule), cost, and risk are on the list—what is most important, second most important, and so forth. Lead your customers into focusing on the high-priority items; don't let them get bogged down in the muck of trivial or less important issues. It's better to be well prepared for a few big issues than to be somewhat

Chapter 3: Gathering Data and Establishing Prenegotiation Objectives

prepared for all possible issues. You should always be prepared to manage conflict, as the team will not always agree on the priorities.

Your next step is to lead the team in arranging these issues in a list from most important to least important—using the customer priorities you helped the team establish. This will give you a prioritized list of issues you want to discuss in the negotiation.

After the list is created and agreed to, draw a line across that list, somewhere near the middle. Everyone must agree on where the line goes. Label all the issues above that line "must" points. All those below the line become "give" points. Must points are those issues that *must* go your way—objectives that must be met or agreement may not be reached. Give points are issues that you are willing to *give* on a little to reach a final agreement. Must points are your gotta haves—they should be the concrete *needs* of the government. Give points are your nice-to-haves, which usually reflect the *wants* of your customer.

After all the issues are labeled, ask your team for a few additional "give" points and add them to the bottom of the list. Price should always be below the line as a give point, because it almost always changes as a result of the give-and-take of negotiation. Both sides usually build in some flexibility on price, and both sides will expect some movement. In addition, tradeoffs on other issues are usually made against price.

In establishing these must and give points, you are building flexibility into your negotiation. Understand that the other side will likely be doing the same thing.

Once you have established and ranked your negotiation priorities and decided on your must and give points, you're ready to finalize your prenegotiation objectives by establishing your acceptable negotiation range for each issue. For each significant issue you'll be negotiating—each issue you have labeled as a must or a give point—you now establish three positions: a minimum position (MIN), a target position (TGT), and a maximum position (MAX). Because you're the buyer, your MIN position should be your best-case scenario—if everything works out exactly like you want it to. Your TGT position is your estimation of the most likely result given the give-and-take of negotiation. It's not all you hoped for, but it's about what you expected, and you can live with it. Your MAX position is the worst-case scenario. That's the point at which you no longer believe the price to be fair and reasonable—your walk-away point. This process builds in more flexibility for your negotiation.

> **Manager Alert**
> Establish three positions: a minimum position (MIN), a target position (TGT), and a maximum position (MAX) for each significant issue you'll be negotiating.

The other side will be doing the same thing; somewhere between your MIN and their MAX, your goals should intersect. It's precisely here—where your range of flexibility intersects with theirs—that the possibility of an agreement exists. This is called the zone of potential agreement.

Chapter 4

RESEARCHING THE OTHER PARTY

Now that we have our objectives down, it's time to collect as much information as we can about what to expect from the other side during the negotiation event. To prepare for the negotiation, you want to get as much general information on the company you'll be dealing with as possible. You'll also want to know as much as possible about the individuals who will be sitting across the table from you and your team.

RESEARCHING THE COMPANY

Do a little research into the company's past negotiation history. Does it have a reputation for driving a hard bargain? Does it tend to use certain negotiation strategies and tactics? How concerned is it about reputation?

What are the company's goals, both long-term and short-term? What does it pride itself on? What are its published core values and vision? Can you get any insight into the company's unstated goals? Sometimes goals on paper are just that; the company may have other unstated priorities that influence how it will act.

Where does it stand, compared to competitors, in the market? Is it a new company? An old company? Is it considered a market leader in the industry? Follower? Innovator? Is it trying to expand into a new market? Is this its first government contract? If not, what percentage of the company's business is with the government? Is it small or large? Is it a subsidiary of a larger company? The answers to all these questions will give you important clues to how the company's negotiators are going to conduct themselves in the negotiation and thus how you should craft your approach to dealing with them.

Try to get insights into the company's cost structure. What is its standard profit margin? How does it price goods or services? Is it profitable? Is it considered the low-priced (and low-quality) leader, or the high-priced icon? Is its business or profit margins expanding or contracting? Is it starved for cash, desperate for business? Is it unionized?

Does the company have standard terms and conditions it habitually adheres to or ask for? What is its discount policy? What kind of warranties does it offer? Does it walk away from deals it perceives to be too risky? Does it have a reputation for trying to "buy-in" on contracts?

RESEARCHING THE COMPANY'S NEGOTIATORS

If you can, you also want to gather as much "intel" as possible on the individual who will be representing the contractor in the negotiation. To find out who that person is, all you need to do is ask the contractor! You could even consider requesting in the solicitation that companies identify this person in their proposals. Once you know who your counterpart is going to be, check out that individual's personal history in previous negotiations. If you haven't had dealings with that person, contact someone who has—another contracting officer, for example, even a contracting officer from a different agency or office. Just check the contractor's past performance information to find out whom to call. Then try to find out as much as you can about the person and how he or she negotiates.

What's his or her company job title? Does he or she even work for the company as an employee or as a professional negotiator brought in on a fee or contingent basis? How many government negotiations has he or she been involved in? What agencies were the contracts for? Is he or she new to the company? New to government negotiations?

Is he or she known for ethical or unethical behavior in the past? Does he or she have a reputation for making concessions or driving a hard bargain? When does the negotiator generally make most concessions—up front, during, or at the end of negotiations? Is he or she a technical subject-matter expert in the function being negotiated? Is he or she prone to making snap judgments?

What kind of negotiation style and tactics is the negotiator known to use? Does he or she change style and tactics frequently or act predictably? Is he or she perceived as using negotiation tricks? If so, which tricks does he or she like to use? Is he or she known to be a talker or a good listener? Does the negotiation tend to dominate conversations and talk about himself or herself? (You can turn this into a *great* advantage at the negotiation table.) Does the negotiator like to take risks or is he or she cautious and risk averse?

As you gather this information on your counterpart and start assessing it, try to put yourself in his or her shoes. How do you think the negotiator views the situation? How do you think he or she perceives you? This exercise—putting yourself in your counterpart's shoes—will help you assimilate all the pieces of information you have collected or observed into a general picture of that negotiator as a real live person. With that picture, you will be in a better position to predict how that individual will act and react in the negotiation room.

> **Manager Alert**
> Anticipate your counterpart's actions by putting yourself in the negotiator's shoes, looking at issues the way you think he or she perceives them.

In a negotiation, information is power; the most informed side is the most prepared side—and that's usually the side that comes out on top. Don't feel bad about researching the other side. If you're up against a professional negotiator, I'll guarantee that he or she is already busy collecting this same information—as much of it as possible—on both your agency and you personally. As you'll see when we discuss some of the tactics that you can employ or that can be employed against you, it is well worth your time to learn everything you can about the other party prior to the negotiation.

INFORMATION SOURCES

Getting information about the other side is not as daunting as it first seems. Plenty of sources are readily available. We have already discussed ways to gather data to help you identify and set your negotiation positions and priorities. Many of these same sources can give you a double bang by providing general clues about the other side. The contractor's proposal, for instance, usually contains useful management summaries that give a glimpse into the company's overall motives, values, and objectives. Also, when you have prenegotiation exchanges with companies to obtain proposal-specific information, use these interactions to research the companies and the negotiators—their attitudes, how they react to certain approaches, how forthcoming they are, how willing to please they are, and the like.

Talk to government customers and technical personnel who have some experience dealing with that company. Certain professions and technical fields develop bonds between their practitioners that can transcend company, and even company/government, boundaries. Based on these ties, these other government folks may know a lot more about the real situation than even their contracting officers do!

A company's publicly available catalogs, brochures, news releases, and the like contain a wealth of useful information. But the best way to get information on the company or the negotiator is one we often overlook—simply ask! We tend to shy away from asking questions, especially ones we don't think will be answered. If that's the case with you, you've got to get over it. We'll give you some tips on how to ask questions effectively in Chapter 10.

Government databases and private for-profit sources can also be useful. Most of these are available on the web. You'll want to check out industry and trade association websites for the particular good or service you're negotiating. Dun and Bradstreet (www.dnb.com) and the Thomas Register (www.thomasregister.com) are good private database services.

Finally, use the Internet. Just punch the company's name into a search engine and you'll be amazed at the information that will pop up. Often, you can get useful results searching on the name of the individual you will be negotiating with. Be sure to also search on the topic (the goods or services) you'll be negotiating for. This search should bring up useful websites such as professional organizations.

INFO-GATHERING TIPS

Many people feel they just don't have the time to do this research. You know you should do it, and you know it will help you do a better negotiation job, but you have these nasty time constraints. What to do? You've simply got to learn to use your limited time wisely. A few shortcuts can help you get to the essential information you need quickly and efficiently.

First, treat researching the other side as a process, not an event. Divide the process into bite-sized chunks. If you set aside, for example, a particular day to cram it all in, you'll get bored and frustrated and consequently miss a lot of important information. Pace yourself. Cut the research into manageable chunks, and stretch it out. *Always* be in information-receive mode.

Second, tailor your research effort to the situation. Your time, energy, and effort have a real dollar cost, not only to you personally but also to your agency and taxpayers. Don't spend an inordinate amount of time doing elaborate research for small-dollar, simple negotiations. Tailor the amount and complexity of your research effort to the dollar value and complexity of what you are negotiating. You can also cut down on effort if you already have experience with the company or its negotiator—or know a trusted source that does. You're an important asset, so try to manage your vital time wisely.

> ### Manager Alert
> Tailor the amount and complexity of your market research effort to the dollar value and complexity of what you are negotiating.

Third, don't be afraid to ask questions directly of the contractor. Most human beings have a natural tendency to help people they consider less informed, less knowledgeable, or even less intelligent than they are. They can't help it—it makes them feel good. An effective way to create this perception is to admit you don't have all the answers. Say things like, "I don't understand your market. What kind of competition do you have?" Admitting you don't know all the answers humanizes you and makes people more receptive to you. Ask open-ended questions to generate not just answers but information.

By the way, once you ask a question, *be quiet!* The vast majority of us aren't great listeners, but it's a habit you need to develop if you want to be a successful negotiator. Resist the urge to elaborate or butt in after you've asked a question. You can't learn anything from talking, only from listening. In addition to the information you asked for, you may pick up unintentional slips, verbal intonations, or a certain emphasis that sends a message quite different from what is actually being said. Train yourself to hear not only what is being said but also what isn't being said. Whether your realize it or not, your negotiation has already begun when you start asking questions and researching the other party.

Manager Alert

Your negotiation has already begun when you start asking questions and researching the other party, so resist the urge to elaborate on your own statements. Train yourself to listen instead of talk.

Chapter 5

DEVELOPING THE NEGOTIATION PLAN

Your negotiation plan is *how* you are going to go about achieving your prenegotiation objectives; it is your blueprint for the actual negotiation event. The quality of your plan directly affects how successful you'll be in the negotiation. Your agency may have a recommended template for a negotiation plan; most good plans will, at a minimum, cover these areas:

- Overall objectives
- Background information
- Team members
- Negotiation objectives
- Major issues
- Negotiation strategy
- Schedule and logistics.

OVERALL OBJECTIVES

The plan should start off by describing the overall objectives of the negotiation. What end are you seeking? A clear, concise objectives statement gives focus to the plan, provides a rallying point for the team, and provides a roadmap for the negotiation. Your statement should be a summary, at a high level, of your overall negotiation objectives e.g., dollars, contract type, financing terms. Your ultimate goal is to get best value at a fair and reasonable price to both parties.

BACKGROUND INFORMATION

Next, include brief background information related to the acquisition, the contractor, and the overall negotiating environment or situation. Most of this information will come from work you have already done—the acquisition plan, the solicitation documents, your market research, your prenegotiation objectives, and your research into the other party. Talk about the general market environment. Discuss the level and amount of competition. List the negotiators for the contractors, their job titles, the contractors' previous history with the government, and the like. Don't be verbose here; a good, brief summary will do.

TEAM MEMBERS

Here you list the names, positions, roles, and responsibilities of the members of your negotiation team. Indicate who will be your technical experts for issues, who will take the lead for each issue, and who will be your actors in carrying out strategy and tactics. Be sure to include a person to keep the minutes of the session. Don't forget to include possible alternate team members in your plan to cover contingencies such as absences. You may also use this section to state that all team members have been properly briefed on procurement integrity, limits on exchanges, limits on authority, nondisclosure of proprietary and source selection information, and ethics.

NEGOTIATION OBJECTIVES

This section states your specific negotiation objectives for each issue. Here, you'll lay out your prenegotiation positions (MIN/MAX/TGT) in priority order, issue by issue. For example, issue #1 will be your most important issue, and you will discuss it completely before moving to issue #2. (Remember to include both your must and your give points.) Keep in mind that you don't have to discuss the issues in this order during the negotiation. The strategy you choose will set the discussion priority.

Then list the contractor's anticipated positions on these issues, laying out the results of your team's technical evaluation of the contractor's proposal for each issue (e.g., strengths, weaknesses, deficiencies). Briefly summarize those positions and cross-reference them back to the technical evaluation report for more detailed information.

Next you'll want to write down your assessment of each side's relative bargaining power for each issue. Examples of bargaining power are level of competition, expertise and knowledge, time constraints, quality and skills of the negotiators, and risks. Writing down your assessment will help you understand how strong you are on each issue. You can even identify potential items within each issue that can be traded off. Price is always considered a tradeoff, but also look at other factors as potential tradeoffs, like delivery dates, FOB points, warranties, financing, and technical considerations.

Also think through and document some preplanned counteroffers for each issue. These should be small tradeoffs you have already considered and discussed with your team that do not detract from your overall position and are comfortably under your target (TGT) position. For instance, providing financing or receiving some technical benefit for a gizmo may not be all that important to you (your give points), but it may be very important to the other side. The ability to give up these things may enable you to receive concessions in return in areas you do care about.

MAJOR ISSUES

This section will highlight important factors that affect the entire negotiation. Include factors that apply to all issues, not just specific ones. Examples include major terms and conditions proposed by the contractors and areas where the government has encouraged the contractors to propose alternative ways of solving a particular problem (e.g., lease vs. purchase). Also discuss any unique aspects of your requirement, such as quality assurance requirements or higher level quality control requirements. List avoidance points (things you don't want anyone on your team to mention) in this section too.

NEGOTIATION STRATEGY

This section will lay out your overall plan to address the issues, conduct the negotiation, and control the negotiation process. Choosing the right strategy is a three-part process. First, you assess each side's bargaining power. Next, you establish your "best alternative to a negotiated agreement" (BATNA). Finally, you select the appropriate strategy based on your assessment of relative power.

Step 1. Assess Bargaining Power

As best you can, determine which side has the most power—the most negotiation leverage—going into the negotiation. Your answer will tell you which negotiation strategy to select. The major categories of bargaining power that can affect negotiations include
- Legitimacy (which side is perceived to be more legitimate?)
- Competition (the more, the better!)
- Time (who has the shorter deadline?)
- Expertise (who knows the business best?)
- Risk tolerance
- Precedent
- Options (have a BATNA).

Step 2. Establish Your BATNA

Your BATNA is your walk-away point, your next best alternative if you cannot reach an acceptable agreement during the negotiation. To develop your BATNA, simply ask yourself, "At what point is it no longer worthwhile to continue negotiating?" Your BATNA is usually somewhere near your bottom line, but it doesn't necessarily have to *be* your bottom line. In competitive negotiations, your BATNA could simply be to go with another offeror's proposal or to cancel the solicitation and resolicit with changes or modifications to your requirement. In noncompetitive negotiations, your BATNA could be to do the work in-house. To establish your BATNA, simply list all your choices short of reaching an agreement with a contractor and pick the best one. That's your BATNA!

> **Manager Alert**
> Your BATNA is your best alternative to a negotiated agreement. It's the best choice to satisfy your need short of an agreement with a contractor.

Your BATNA serves as a standard against which to measure any proposed agreement. It prevents you from accepting an agreement with unfavorable terms. Comparing the other side's proposed solution against your BATNA can also give you clues on what to counter with to improve the terms of agreement. Finally, going into a negotiation already knowing what you will do if you fail to reach agreement can make you a more confident negotiator. You have created at least one alternative for your side.

Step 3. Select Your Strategy

There are four basic strategies you can choose:
- WIN-LOSE strategy
- Loss prevention strategy (also known as defensive strategy)
- WIN-WIN strategy
- WIN-win strategy (that's big win-little win).

1. **WIN-LOSE strategy**. This classic strategy sets you up to win at the expense of the other side. Although not preferred by government negotiators, this strategy has its place. Use it when your assessment of relative power reveals that you have the preponderance of power. As long as you can find a price that is fair and reasonable to both sides, you're free to use WIN-LOSE as a strategy. This is particularly true if you perceive the contractor's going-in position to be unreasonable. When using

the WIN-LOSE approach, have a firm going in position—and a limit beyond which you won't go.

2. Loss prevention strategy. Loss prevention is a defensive strategy you'll use only if you perceive that the other side has the predominant balance of power—for example, in sole source negotiations or negotiations for modifications to existing contracts. If the balance of power is definitely in the other side's favor, you can take some strategic actions.

First, arrange your issues in the order of least to greatest importance to you. You can also arrange them by your perception of ease of agreement. This gets the other side used to saying "yes." Next, try to create options. Don't immediately sacrifice your goals—try to expand them, or explore other ways to get to them. Put the phrase "what if" in front of your issues. If you don't think you can win on one point, bring in several points that may set up both of you as winners.

Finally, don't forget your BATNA. In loss prevention, you sometimes just have to walk away. As a matter of fact, in government contracting, you must *never* agree to a price or arrangement that you, as a contracting officer, do not find fair and reasonable.

3. WIN-WIN strategy. Here you focus on interests rather than positions. Both sides work together to satisfy each other's needs. You also use open communication to share your needs with each other. You collaborate to make the "pie" bigger so everyone wins. You don't try to use relative power against each other. Both parties realize that they have shared objectives, not mutually exclusive positions. The strategic points that naturally follow are as follows:

- A focus on mutual interests, not mutually exclusive and conflicting positions
- Effective listening to determine the interests behind the positions
- Working together, not against each other, to come up with creative solutions.

But—and this is crucial—for the WIN-WIN strategy to work, both parties have to play by the WIN-WIN rules. This presents serious obstacles to putting the WIN-WIN strategy to use in the government contracting arena. Federal law often precludes truly innovative WIN-WIN solutions, with restrictions on long-term investment, multiple-contract deals, and innovative cash flow solutions such as contract financing and advance payment. So, WIN-WIN is an ideal, but in reality it's a rarity in its pure form in government contract negotiations.

4. WIN-win strategy (big win for you, little win for them)

This is a variant of the WIN-WIN strategy outlined by Ron Shapiro, Mark Jankowski, and James Dale, in their book, *The Power of Nice* (Wiley & Sons, 2001). In WIN-win, we achieve all or most of our goals while letting the other side achieve some of their goals. You satisfy your interests well and their interests acceptably.

The WIN-win negotiation approach involves
- Never making the first offer
- Never accepting the first offer
- Satisfying the contractor's true interests but not at the expense of *your* goals!

SCHEDULE AND LOGISTICS

Here you draw up your anticipated schedule of events leading up to and ending in a completed negotiation, indicating anticipated times for major milestones along the way. You also address logistics issues—those little details that can create or frustrate a smooth negotiation event. Make sure to check your agency directives for any approvals that may be required, and build them into your schedule.

Insist on conducting the negotiation event at your facility—*you want home court advantage*! Note in the plan who will take the official negotiation minutes, making sure it's someone from the government side. As far as the physical site, make sure

- The room is large enough.
- Lighting is adequate.
- There are enough chairs, and they are comfortable.
- Table space is adequate.
- Audiovisual equipment is set up and working if it is needed.
- A second room is available for private caucuses.
- There is easy access to phones, computer lines, etc.
- Paper, pencils, and pens are available for each attendee, and extras are available. Essentials like coffee, snacks, restrooms, etc., are available.
- Water, ice, and drinking glasses are available in the room.
- A large wall clock can be seen by everyone in the room.
- Parking spaces and passes are prearranged for the other side's team members.
- Escorts are available in secure or classified areas and will be available for the other side during breaks.

> **Manager Alert**
> Insist on conducting the negotiation event at your facility—*you want home court advantage*!

Chapter 5: Developing the Negotiation Plan   23

Once you make all these arrangements, include them in your negotiation plan and make sure all your team members have a copy so everyone knows what's going on. Review the plan with your team and ask for input. Make sure everyone understands their role. Go over some negotiation "do's and don'ts," using Federal Acquisition Regulation (FAR 15) and your personal experience as guides. If you have time, rehearse by conducting a mock negotiation with your team members. Appoint someone to act as the opposition, and have them try to poke holes in your negotiation positions.

Chapter 6

DEVELOPING THE NEGOTIATION AGENDA

After you have finished your negotiation preparations and rehearsed the plan, your next step is to develop an agenda for the actual negotiation session. The agenda is a critical tool for getting the negotiations started right—and asserting control over the pace and the process. The agenda will also be how you let the other side know critical things like location, time, and access requirements without giving them your entire negotiation plan.

The agenda should first cover general information such as time, location, breaks, duration, points of contact, and seating capacity. Next, list the negotiation issues you plan to discuss in the priority that supports your strategy. You should then send the agenda to the contractor in draft form, labeling it a "proposed agenda." Make sure to give the contractor enough time to respond.

When you send out your draft agenda, ask who the lead negotiator will be and what authority he or she has to finalize any agreements or changes you decide on during the negotiation session. Ask how many people will attend the negotiation, who these folks will be, and what expertise they represent. The main reason is to make sure you have enough chairs, refreshments, and the like, to accommodate them. Another reason is to make sure your team matches their expertise—person for person.

When you get your draft agenda back from the other side, with or without comments, you can finalize the agenda. Any comments that come back on your draft agenda will give you additional insights into the other side. If the contractor has provided comments or suggestions, you don't necessarily have to change your agenda—that's totally your call. Remember, you control the process.

Update your agenda as you like and change it from "draft" to "final." Make sure to provide a copy to everyone who will attend the negotiation session on your side, as well as to key members of your supporting cast who may not actually participate in the negotiation (e.g., program staff), the contractor, and your boss.

> **Manager Alert**
> Ask how many people will attend the negotiation, who these folks will be, and what expertise they represent. The main reason is to make sure you have enough chairs, refreshments, and the like to accommodate them. Another reason is to make sure your team matches their expertise—person for person.

Chapter 7

ASSIGNING NEGOTIATION ROLES

Many negotiation experts agree that the ideal negotiation team should consist of three to five people. The five traditional roles that team members can assume for a negotiation are team leader, good cop, bad cop, technocrat, and sweeper. Each of these roles should be well-defined and practiced.

Some people are natural picks to play certain roles. More than one role may be assigned to one person, as long as the roles don't conflict. If you're the only negotiator, obviously you'll have to assume at least the key responsibilities of all the roles. Even if you prefer not to assign roles, you still should be familiar with them because the other side will probably assign similar roles to its own team members.

TEAM LEADER

The team leader should be the person with the most negotiating experience, not necessarily the most senior person on the team. The contracting officer most often fills this role. The team leader opens the negotiation, sets the tone, controls the team, controls all communication by members of the team, calls caucuses, decides tough calls, breaks deadlocks, sets and directs all other actions by team members, and concludes and summarizes the negotiation. The team leader controls the agenda and the process and is responsible for the results of the negotiation.

The team leader must be strong and resolute—and must be viewed as such by the other side. However, the team leader should not be too dictatorial or rigid. Only a seasoned negotiator can split this difference well.

If you are short-handed, the team leader may have to assume other roles as well, the most important probably being the responsibilities of the sweeper. Try not to have your team leader play the role of bad cop, however; your team leader should always be perceived as fair to the other side.

GOOD COP

The ideal person to fill the role of good cop is someone who is naturally likeable and whose outgoing personality easily draws people. The good cop expresses sympathy and understanding for the other side's position and views, becoming someone the other side can identify with. He or she creates a bond with the other side's team members. The members of the other side consider him or her at least one person on your team who sees things their way and is someone they can trust. This image gradually builds and strengthens as the negotiation progresses.

Of course, it's all a well-calculated tactic. The good cop is simply playing a role intended to lull the other side into a false sense of security. Soon the contractor doesn't mind sharing tidbits of information with this "sympathetic" person that it wouldn't dare share with anyone else on your team; this trust enables you to pick up critical information that can affect the negotiation significantly. More importantly, the good cop sets the stage to serve as a foil for the bad cop when you're ready to use the good cop/bad cop tactic.

> **Manager Alert**
> The good cop's role is to lull the other side into a false sense of security so its negotiators will talk more freely and disclose more information.

Since the good cop complements and plays off the role of the bad cop, both their roles must be planned and rehearsed well in advance of the negotiation. If you're short-handed, the roles and responsibilities of good cop can be assumed by either the team leader or the sweeper.

BAD COP

The bad cop's role is to play someone who is nasty to deal with—negative, confrontational, intimidating, constantly arguing, and always opposed to everything the other side says. Many government teams use a technical or program person, maybe even the program manager, to play the role of bad cop. The other side usually picks an accountant or lawyer to play the role.

The bad cop's job is to riddle the other side's positions with objections and undermine its progress. He or she is also in an excellent position to throw contentious issues or extreme positions on the table without jeopardizing the apparent objectivity and fairness of the other members of her team. The bad cop can be used to employ delaying tactics, emotional tactics, and the walkout tactic.

Since the other side never knows when the bad cop is going to blow up next, he keeps the opposing team off balance.

The bad cop's most important role is to set up the good cop to be effective in the good cop/bad cop tactic. His or her negative conduct enables your good cop to establish rapport with the other side. Your good cop plays the role of opposing or trying to moderate the conduct of your bad cop, drawing the other side to your good cop. The contractor becomes more willing to share information with or make concessions directly to your good cop, who seems to understand their needs.

If you're short-handed, the technocrat can double as the bad cop. Someone outside the negotiating room can also play the bad cop. Just don't assign the bad cop role to the sweeper or team leader.

TECHNOCRAT

Also called the confuser or hard liner, the technocrat's role is to confuse the other side by continuously interjecting facts, figures, or data that may or may not be pertinent to the issue being discussed. He or she complicates matters, throws things off track, and gives the other side additional points to address, defend, or explain. The technocrat comes into the room heavily laden with files, folders, and printouts. He or she spreads these all around and refers to them constantly during negotiations. The technocrat is always working a calculator and repeatedly asks to see and verify the other side's facts and figures. The technocrat is not as nasty or ill-mannered as the bad cop, but he or she takes a hard line and challenges the other side's facts, figures, and assumptions. He or she exudes an aura of intelligence and is often deferred to by other team members, even the team lead.

The technocrat can drag out the negotiation if that is part of your plan. She doesn't let the members of the other side relax—constantly forcing them to validate their numbers or justify their positions. He or she can even challenge your own team member's facts, figures, and assumptions, allowing your team to retreat from positions that appear too generous.

> **Manager Alert**
> The technocrat confuses members of the other side with facts and figures, not letting them relax and constantly forcing them to validate their numbers or justify their positions.

Assign the technocrat role to someone who's naturally analytical. If you need to double up, the technocrat's role can be assumed by your bad cop or, in a pinch, your team leader.

SWEEPER

The sweeper's main job is to listen and observe. At crucial moments, the sweeper will finally speak up to summarize the many different points of view and issues into one consolidated picture. He or she may then suggest a way forward from that point. The sweeper keeps the negotiation free from bogging down on small issues or from straying too far off the subject. Common phrases for a sweeper include, "So what I hear you saying is…," "Let me see if I can put this all together…," and "I hear what your side is saying. I hear what our side is saying. How about we consider doing…." In essence, the sweeper "sweeps" up all the crumbs and bits of what's going on and assembles them in one pile.

Another important duty of the sweeper is to observe and soak in. The sweeper strategically seated at the end of the negotiating table for a reason. From that position, he or she can look lengthwise down the table at the other side's team members. He or she can gauge the other side's reactions to your team's positions. The sweeper is better able to pick up on subtle gestures the other side's team members make, such as a quick kick in the leg under the table. During a caucus or break, the sweeper will report these observations to the team, providing extremely valuable information.

The ideal candidate for the important role of sweeper is someone with a good personality but a somewhat reserved disposition. The sweeper needs to be organized and good at seeing the big picture. Finally, he or she needs to be highly observant by nature. If you're short-handed, sweeper duties can be picked up by your good cop, the team leader, or even the technocrat.

Chapter 8

USING TACTICS IN NEGOTIATIONS

As a government negotiator, you must be fair and reasonable; while there are many effective negotiation tactics you can use, there are some you simply can't use. These tactics (good *and* unethical) can be used against you, however, so you must be aware of and understand them. If you recognize them for what they are when they're used against you, you will be able to employ possible countermoves to negate their effect.

Tactics are a natural part of negotiation, and not all tactics are bad or manipulative. It is not only okay for you to use tactics as a government negotiator, but the FAR encourages you to do so. FAR 15.3 requires that when you conduct contracting by negotiations, you hold "discussions" with all offerors in the competitive range. The FAR goes on to say that these discussions may include bargaining. What the FAR doesn't tell you is *how* to bargain. Your job as a government negotiator is to get a fair and reasonable conclusion for the taxpayers. Negotiation tactics will help you achieve that goal.

> **Manager Alert**
> Your job as a government negotiator is to get a fair and reasonable conclusion for the taxpayers. Negotiation tactics will help you achieve that goal.

My primary purpose in showing you the tactics you can and can't use is to make you a better government negotiator. After all, you are responsible for spending my tax money, and I therefore have a personal vested interest in your doing your job effectively. These tactics are universal, so understanding how to use and counter them can also help you in any personal negotiation situation you encounter in your daily life—buying a house, a car, or a major appliance, for example.

So let's start with the tactics that you, as a government negotiator, can use. We'll then turn to those tactics you can't use but need to understand and counter.

Chapter 9

TIME TACTICS

Time can be a friend or a foe. The two key tactics related to time are time pressure and time investment.

THE TIME PRESSURE TACTIC

If one side is under time pressure to come to an agreement quickly, it gives the other side tremendous negotiating power. If you are on the side that has the time advantage, you can use time as a very effective pressure tactic. The secret to using time pressure as a tactic is to find out the other side's deadline (everyone has one) while not letting them figure out *your* deadline. This is important because most significant concessions in any negotiation will come very close to the deadline. People faced with a deadline tend to procrastinate, and everyone tends to become a lot more flexible when confronted with time pressure.

> **Manager Alert**
> Most significant concessions in any negotiation will come very close to the deadline.

Contractors use time pressure against the government by trying to get a negotiation session postponed until a Friday—preferably the Friday before a three-day federal holiday. They know the government negotiators will be under tremendous time pressure to reach a deal—even if it's not the best deal they could have held out for—so the negotiation won't drag on into a Saturday and ruin their weekend plans.

What factors can make time pressure work against you? How about expiring funds or a customer who *has* to have what the contractor is offering by a certain date? How about key members of your team who won't be available after a certain date? Or maybe your own supervisor has put a deadline on you and told you not to come back without a deal. These are all realities you might have to deal with, but under no circumstances let the other side know about them. Act like you have all the time in the world to reach agreement. That will throw the pressure back on them because they have a deadline too.

It's okay for you to use time pressure as a tactic. Even if you can't find out the other side's deadline, remember that they do have one. Their bosses probably have given them marching orders to come back with a deal by a certain time. Maybe they need to win this contract by a certain date to solve a cash flow problem or to make a quarterly earnings report look better for their stockholders. Maybe they have another important negotiation coming up that they want their negotiators free to take on.

You can effectively use the tactic of time pressure in every negotiation simply by holding your major issues until late in the negotiation. Be patient. Don't fire all your guns at once. Let time pressure work for you, not against you.

COUNTERS TO THE TIME PRESSURE TACTIC

If the other side is attempting to use time pressure against you, the best counter is to simply recognize it for what it is—a tactic. That puts you back in control and negates the emotional effect the contractor hopes the tactic will have on you. Let their negotiators know politely that you won't be pressured by time. Let them know that you know they're using a tactic. Getting caught using a tactic could even embarrass the other side so much that it will throw you a free concession!

Another effective counter is to tie up all the preliminary negotiation details, including the time allotted for the negotiation, up front. Use your agenda. As the negotiation progresses and agreements are reached on issues, tie up the details of the agreements as you go. That reduces the room the other side has to drag the negotiation on as a way of applying pressure. Never agree to "work out the details later." Work them out *now* and put them in writing as you agree to them.

> **Manager Alert**
> Never agree to "work out the details later." Work them out *now* and put them in writing as you agree to them.

Finally, use your BATNA as a safety valve against time pressure. Never be forced to go lower than your BATNA because of time pressure. That's why you have a BATNA—to protect you from getting so caught up in the negotiation that you come away with a bad deal. Never be afraid to pull the plug if you reach your BATNA.

THE TIME INVESTMENT TACTIC

Closely related to the time pressure tactic is the time investment tactic. Two principles come into play. First, the longer you can keep the other side negotiating, the more likely its negotiators will be to move toward your point of view. Slowly, over time, their minds change and their initial positions soften. Second, the more personal time, energy, and effort negotiators put into the process, the more anxious they become to reach a deal. They don't want all the time and effort to go to waste. They have made an investment of time in you and want something to show for it—even if it isn't everything initially sought.

Time is money to contractors, so the tactic of time investment usually works well on them. Their negotiators are valuable assets to the company who are expensive to use, and they need to move on to the next deal. The more time they have invested in the negotiation, the more motivated they are not to come back empty handed. The balance of power shifts to you.

COUNTERS TO THE TIME INVESTMENT TACTIC

If this tactic is used against you, your best counter is to totally disregard your "sunk" time. **Don't let sunk time bother you.** You will like have already invested time before you even recognize the tactic; mentally, you just have to write it off. Know when to say when if it won't be productive to continue the negotiation in its current state. Remember your BATNA and let it protect you from getting pulled down a nonproductive trail—tying up yet more time and money—just because you have already invested so much time in the negotiation.

Chapter 10

QUESTION AND TRIAL BALLOON TACTICS

You can use questions and trial balloons to scope out the other side's true priorities and "give" points.

THE QUESTION TACTIC

In any negotiation, knowledge is power. You increase your power relative to the other side as you increase your knowledge about it. Use questions to probe for answers that will increase your information about the other side. Dig for more information about its position, interests, needs, hidden agendas, and so forth. In a negotiation, acting dumb is smart! When you ask questions, you tap into the tendency for people to want to help out folks they regard as less informed or less intelligent than they are. It makes them feel important.

> **Manager Alert**
> In a negotiation, acting dumb is smart! Asking questions taps into the tendency for people to want to help out when they regard someone as less informed or less intelligent than they are.

So ask questions that make the other side feel superior, such as, "I'm not sure I fully grasp all the intricacies in your proposal. Would you mind explaining them to me again?" Or, "I know the dollars you are proposing are backed up with sound facts, but for some reason I'm just not getting it. Can you explain to me how you came up with these figures?" Notice that you are asking for help in both these examples. Get in the habit of asking that all-important question, "Can you help me…?" That's almost guaranteed to trigger the human need for the other side to feel smart and superior, and the negotiators will give you information they otherwise wouldn't have. You also should use questions to test the credibility of the "facts" the other side is asserting.

Get good at asking open-ended questions that start with "how," "what," "what else," "which," and "why." Some examples include the following: "*How did you come up with those figures?*" The negotiators now have to defend their position with additional facts, and remember, any additional information shifts power. "*What would you do if you were in my shoes and someone gave you that choice?*" This has the added benefit of bringing them around to your side, even if it's just a little bit. "*What is really important to you?*" Always follow up with "*what else is important?*" If they see you as caring for their position, they are likely to be more open sharing information with you. Then, ask them "*which of these things is more important to you?*" This gives you insight into their "must" and "give" positions. Test their credibility by asking "*why do you think that position is fair?*" That puts them on the defensive to justify their position.

Notice that all these questions are open ended and can't be answered by a simple "yes" or "no" or with some finite fact. These questions require elaboration, which will give you more information. Closed-ended questions run the risk of eliciting a simple answer and nothing more. For example, if you ask, "Don't you think your price is a little too high?" the contractor may answer with a simple "no." That doesn't give you much information. If you ask "when will you be able to deliver?" the contractor can answer with one date. Again, you aren't gaining useful information. Get in the habit of asking open-ended questions!

Also practice parroting. For example, if the negotiators say "your required delivery date is unrealistic," simply regurgitate their own statement back at them in the form of a question. In this case, say "You feel our delivery date is unrealistic?" The way they answer that question could give you important insight into what they're thinking. Notice I didn't ask "why" they felt our delivery date was bad—that sometimes throws up warning flags. I simply restated their assertion in the form of a question using the word "feel."

That simple word "feel" can be important to add to your vocabulary. If the negotiators say something like "our standard company policy is never to offer extended warranties," simply respond with "and how do you feel about that policy?" Sometimes this type of question can smoke out whether or not there is any give in the position.

After you ask a question, be silent and wait for the answer. Avoid the temptation to elaborate. If you do, you negate the effect of pulling info from the other side by asking the question. To make matters worse, now more information is flowing *from* your side instead of the other way around. Silence is golden, and it's also a crucial skill you have to work at developing to be a successful negotiator.

> **Manager Alert**
> After you ask a question, be silent and wait for the answer.

THE TRIAL BALLOON TACTIC

You use the tactic of constructing a trial balloon by simply putting "What if..." in front of a statement. Trial balloons relax the other side, making the negotiators feel more free to discuss even issues they may consider "off the table." For example, suppose the other side has strict marching orders not to agree to anything shorter than a 30-day delivery time. You're aware of this, but you need quicker delivery. If you hit them with statements like "I think you need to show some flexibility on delivery date," "We think you should deliver earlier," or "Your delivery time is unacceptable," they will just dig their heels in.

So use a trial balloon. Ask, "What if we had an earlier delivery date?" The use of "we" instead of "you" makes it "our" problem instead of "their" problem. More importantly, the "what if" takes the pressure off the other side—it's just a "what if"! You aren't asking them to commit; you're not directly challenging them. With the pressure off, they're a lot more likely to open up. Now you're likely to find out exactly why they're committed to a 30-day time frame and whether they have any flexibility on the issue.

COUNTERS TO QUESTION AND TRIAL BALLOON TACTICS

The other side also knows that information is power and that asking questions increases information. Thus, you may find yourself barraged with open-ended questions and trial balloons from their negotiators. Questions are a normal part of every negotiation, so the other side doesn't always have sinister intentions by questioning you. But if you think they're digging by questioning and trial-ballooning you to death as a tactic, try these counters.

First, trump them. You do this simply by answering questions with a question of your own. After the negotiators finish asking their question or throwing their trial balloon, say "Can you restate that?" "I don't think I understand. Can you explain?" or "Let me see if I've got this right.... is that correct?" All these responses require an answer—and answering will throw them out of the question mode.

If that doesn't work, try silence: Simply don't answer their question! Silence can get uncomfortable, and the other side might start elaborating on the question or trial balloon to fill the silence. Information is now once again flowing from the other side to you, and that's what you want.

Chapter 11

THE SILENCE TACTIC

Most people are uncomfortable with silence, so you can use silence as a tactic in negotiations. After you make a point, simply *be silent*. More importantly, after the other side makes a point or asks a question, be silent and wait. If you don't answer immediately, the negotiators for the other side are likely to continue to talk and elaborate. And when they do, they'll either modify their position and give you more concessions or at least give you more information than you had before. It's human nature!

Of course, human nature applies to you as well. Fight the temptation to jump in with your views or opinions, especially if what they're saying is wrong or you don't agree. Good negotiators are better listeners than talkers. Simply wait the negotiators for the other side out in silence and see how many times they'll modify their positions without your having to say a word.

> **Manager Alert**
> Your silence can cause the negotiators for the other side to modify their positions without your having to say a word.

Salespeople are taught a tactic called the "silent close." For example, after going back and forth with you, a car salesperson will sigh, write a number down on a piece of paper, push it over to you, and say something like "this is the absolute best I can do." Then he or she is silent. As a general rule, the next person to talk loses. Great negotiators will let you ramble on as much as possible once you start talking—even after you have accepted the deal. They're not being courteous. They're not awestruck at the logic of your argument or your brilliance. They're using the silent tactic on you!

COUNTERS TO THE SILENCE TACTIC

The silence tactic is hard to counter. You can always elect to "fight fire with fire" and give the silent treatment right back. Simply refuse to be the first one to talk. If you feel you can't stand it any longer and you absolutely *must* break the silence, you're safest by saying something like, "Excuse me, I have to take a break." Leave the room for a while. When you reconvene, you've increased the likelihood that the other side will break the silence first.

Another counter is one that can be used effectively against every tactic: Simply let the other side know you recognize that it is using the tactic on you. You might say something like, "Hey, you're really great at using the silence tactic. See, you got me to talk first. But since I'm talking, let me ask you, what do you really think of this proposal?" And then *shut up*. See what you've done here? You've countered the silence tactic with your own use of the question tactic—coupled with your own silence tactic!

Another counter to try is not to answer with words. For example, if the car salesperson pushes that piece of paper to you and clams up, get your own piece of paper out, write something on it, and push it back. In this case, you might write "why?" or "too high" or "extras?" If you've made the proposal and are getting the silent treatment, you might write "decision?" or "do you understand?" All these beg a response, don't they? And they all encourage the other side to be the first to break the silence.

Just remember, the more information you have, the more power shifts to you in a negotiation. You can only increase the information you have by being silent and listening, not by talking.

Manager Alert
The more information you have, the more power shifts to you in a negotiation.

Chapter 12

THE VISE TACTIC

The vise tactic, introduced by Roger Dawson in his book *Secrets of Power Negotiating* (Career Press, 2001), is simply using the phrase "You'll have to do better than that." After the other side has presented you with an offer, use the vise tactic. Even if the offer or counteroffer is generous, respond by saying "You'll have to do better than that." This almost always gets you extra concessions you weren't expecting. After you say it, be quiet! Immediately follow up the vise tactic with the silence tactic.

> **Manager Alert**
> Even if their offer or counteroffer is generous, respond by saying "You'll have to do better than that."

To make the tactic more effective, visibly flinch in reaction to the other side's proposal as you employ the vise tactic. Cock your head, pull your shoulders back, and draw some air in through your teeth. Then say "You'll have to do better than that." A flinch shows resistance and puts the other side on notice that it may be pushing too far.

COUNTERS TO THE VISE TACTIC

Just like the vise tactic is one phrase, the counter to it is also one simple phrase. If the other side says "You'll have to do better than that," immediately ask "Exactly how much better do I have to do?"

Chapter 13

THE ORDER-OF-ISSUES TACTIC

Ordering your issues in a certain way in your draft agenda can serve as an effective probe to gain more information about the other side. I can also be an essential part of your negotiation strategy. If your analysis of relative power shows that you have more power than the other side, you'll probably pick big win-little win as a strategy. To support that strategy, arrange your issues in the order of greatest importance to *you*. This sets the tone of the negotiation early—essentially saying to the other side, "Give me this and I'll see what I can do about some of your concerns later." You then can be magnanimous and flexible on some issues that are further down your wish list.

If you are in a position of less power than the other side, say you're in a sole-source negotiation, you can choose to arrange your issues in order of either least to most importance or ease of agreement.

If you put your least important issues first, you can afford to let the other side say "no" to those issues. This benefits you in two ways. First, these issues weren't high on your "must-have" list anyway. Second, the other side will likely be open to reciprocating, especially after they have "won" the first few "victories." The other side may even convince itself that it has already won the negotiation, so the later points won't matter that much. Remember, only *you* know what your priorities are.

Alternatively, you can arrange your issues in order of ease of agreement. You should already have a good idea which issues will be tough to agree to and which will be a breeze. Put the easy ones first on the agenda. That gets the other side in the habit of saying that magic word "yes." The more people say "yes," the more reluctant—even subconsciously—they become to say "no." Arranging issues in order of ease of agreement conditions the other side to saying "yes" and increases the chance it will continue to do so when you get to your most important issues.

> **Manager Alert**
> The more people say "yes," the more reluctant—even subconsciously—they become to say "no."

COUNTERS TO THE ORDER-OF-ISSUES TACTIC

You may not have to counter this tactic at all. You represent the government, and the government sets the agenda for negotiations, including ordering the issues to negotiate. This is a tactic that can be used almost exclusively by the government team.

Don't assume, though, that contractors won't try to take over the agenda-setting process to force their issues on you in the order *they* want. Just stand firm and remain in control of the agenda and you won't have to worry about countering this tactic. Simply don't give the other side a chance to use it.

Chapter 14

THE GOOD COP/ BAD COP TACTIC

This is probably the most commonly used tactic in negotiations, and most people are familiar with it. Even so, it's still one of the best ways to apply pressure to the other side without risking the negative effects of a direct confrontation.

You're probably familiar with the good cop/bad cop tactic from TV shows. Two officers question a suspect together. One officer (the bad cop) is nasty, uncooperative, and threatens the suspect with all kinds of things unless he or she cooperates. As this is going on, the second officer (the good cop) is sitting back, being quiet, and looking mortified that the partner is acting so badly. Suddenly, the first officer is mysteriously called out of the room, sometimes storming out in anger. That leaves the suspect alone in the room with the good cop. This detective is the nicest person in the world. He or she apologizes to the suspect for the partner's behavior and does everything possible to make the suspect feel at ease.

In fact, both officers are playing well-rehearsed roles. If the good cop plays the role right, the suspect starts to feel that the detective is on his or her side. That makes the suspect feel free to share more information than probably intended. The good cop curries favor by being sympathetic and understanding. The good cop is effective because of the previous actions of the bad cop.

The good cop/bad cop tactic can be even more effective when used in combination with other tactics. For example, you can combine it with the time pressure tactic to go something like this:

> "Well, if it were up to me, I'd really like to agree to your terms, Mr. Contractor. I personally think they're reasonable. But my supervisor was pretty upset at your price. In fact, she's already looking for other options right now, like government performance. If I can't bring her back something she thinks is a more reasonable price, she'll likely scrap contracting this project altogether."

COUNTERS TO THE GOOD COP/BAD COP TACTIC

Since this is an overused tactic, the best counter is to let the other side know you see it for what it is—a tactic. "Oh, I get it! You're playing good cop/bad cop on me. Let me guess...who's the good cop?" Or, "I know your accountant is here to play bad cop, but let's stop with the games. I really want to get down to solving this problem in a mutually beneficial way." Call their game and let them know in a nice way that you won't be had.

Another counter is to create a bad cop of your own. If the other side brings a lawyer or accountant to play bad cop, stop the negotiation as soon as you recognize the tactic. Say something like, "Well, since your lawyer feels that way, I really think we should adjourn until I can get our lawyer here in the negotiation to represent us." Then bring in your own bad cop lawyer. Make sure you brief your lawyer first, so he or she knows what's going on.

A third counter is to reverse their playing of good cop/bad cop right back at them. For their tactic to work, their good and bad cops will have to either disagree or at least take different approaches in front of you. Wait until the negotiators start their routine and then say something like, "Whoa! Looks to me like your own team might have some differences of opinion on this. Maybe you weren't as prepared for this negotiation as I thought. Tell you what. I'll let you take a break to see if you can bring your team to some kind of agreement on this issue."

Chapter 15

THE CAUCUS TACTIC

Caucuses are expected in negotiations. You can, however, turn caucuses into an effective negotiation tactic. You can either use the caucus tactic by itself or combine it with other negotiation tactics.

A caucus, for instance, can be used as a strategic break. Calling a caucus when the other side is on a roll can break its momentum and throw its whole game plan out of sync.

> **Manager Alert**
> Calling a caucus can break the other side's momentum and throw its whole game plan out of sync.

You can also use a caucus to keep control of your own team. One of your teammates may say too much, disclose facts you're not ready to disclose, start getting angry and out of control, or start disagreeing with other team members in front of the other side. At that point, call a caucus. Get your team out of the room, give them a lecture, and get them back under control.

Caucuses can also be used to keep control of the pace of negotiations. You want the other side not only to know, but to feel, that you are in charge. If things start going too fast for your game plan, slow the process down by calling a caucus. If you are presented with facts you weren't expecting or a premature offer that changes your strategy, call a caucus to get back in control.

Caucuses are also effective immediately after you receive an offer or counteroffer from the other side. That's when your team is most vulnerable. Undisciplined or untrained team members may blurt out counteroffers or express views on the merits or concerns of the offer. Usually, these comments are not coordinated with the rest of your team and can damage your position. To prevent this, call a caucus immediately after the other side presents its offer or position. This allows your team to think through the offer calmly and privately. When you come back in, you have a consolidated *team* response to the offer without breaking your game plan.

> **Manager Alert**
> Call a caucus immediately after the other side presents its offer or position, allowing your team to think through the offer calmly and privately. When you come back in, you have a consolidated *team* response to the offer without breaking your game plan.

COUNTERS TO THE CAUCUS TACTIC

Simply being the government team sets you up automatically to counter the caucus tactic if you feel it's being used against you. You control the negotiation rules and you run the agenda—including calling the breaks. If the other side asks for a break or a caucus, you have the power to say "No, let's continue until we get this issue sorted out."

Chapter 16

THE NIBBLE TACTIC

Nibbling is asking for a little more after the other side thinks the deal is closed. The nibbler attempts to gain a few extra concessions via little infringements on the terms the other side already thinks are agreed on. For example, a car salesperson, after spending hours trying to sell you a car, finally has you committed to a price. When he or she pushes the papers to you to sign, you pick them up, look at them, wrinkle your brow, and ask, "What type of floor mats are you going to throw in for free? And you know how important underbody rust proofing is in this part of the country, don't you?" That's a nibble.

Three important things make nibbling a successful tactic. First, nibbling is only effective if it's used later in the negotiation, usually right at the end. In fact, the success of the nibble tactic is directly proportional to the amount of time the other side has invested in the deal. The salesperson has just invested hours of commissionable time on you at the expense of closing other deals. He or she is not likely to let you walk for the price of a couple of floor mats and get zero for all the effort.

Second, nibble tactics have to be planned in advance. You've got to purposely hold something back to use as a nibble later. Never ask for everything up front—you'll have nothing left to nibble with. The give points you developed when you were planning your negotiation strategy are always ripe issues to throw in as nibbles. You're happy if you get them, but you won't be crushed if the other side successfully counters your nibble.

> **Manager Alert**
> Use your low-value "give" points as nibbles.

Finally, the nibble ties into people's innate tendency to want to reinforce decisions they have already made. They are emotionally involved in the deal and the last thing they wants is to back out of something they have already set their mind on. In fact, they might not mind caving a little here and there to keep the deal intact. That's how nibbling can be effective in getting concessions late in the game that otherwise would not have been possible or would have taken much more give and take.

Here's an example of how to use the nibble tactic as a government negotiator. Say you're negotiating with a company to buy computer equipment for your office. In your negotiation planning, you identified an extended warranty as one of your "give" points, but it was high on your "nice to have" list. You also know the other side rarely agrees to anything other than its standard commercial warranty. Extended warranties, if they are available at all, come with a hefty price tag. Invest time in the negotiation, giving and taking, and finally come to what the contractor thinks is a meeting of the minds. Right before you shake hands, nibble: "Since the government is one of your biggest customers, I'm assuming we're on your most favored customer list. How many months over your standard commercial warranty have we just bought?"

COUNTERS TO THE NIBBLE TACTIC

Nibbling is a fairly common tactic, and it is highly effective because you are at your most vulnerable when you think the negotiation is done. The nibble plays on the time you've invested in the negotiation, so use the counters you've already learned to the time investment tactic: Disregard "sunk" time, know your BATNA (when to walk away), and tie up all the details of the negotiation up front or as you reach agreement on each issue.

Another counter is to visibly flinch when the other side hits you with the nibble. Flinching not only shows your disappointment at the last-minute change to terms but also signals that the nibble may cost the other side something. After you flinch, take your team out for a caucus. Come back in with a written statement of what the other side will have to give up to get the nibble. In other words, demand a reciprocal concession.

Finally, you can use the ambiguous authority tactic (talked about in the next chapter) to counter the nibble. Simply say something like, "You know, this is something new. I don't think I have the authority to authorize this extra. I didn't know this would come up, so I haven't briefed my boss that this would be part of the deal. I'll have to check with her and get back to you."

Chapter 17

THE AMBIGUOUS AUTHORITY TACTIC

You can use the ambiguous authority tactic when you are the chief negotiator but you don't have ultimate authority to finalize the deal. You may have to go through an approval process before finalizing the negotiated agreement. You may have instructions to consult with a higher-up before you finalize the deal. These people or committees will be the ambiguous authorities you will defer to if you elect to use this tactic.

The most common use of this tactic is in buying a car. You've slogged it out with the salesperson all day and finally think you have a deal. But then the salesperson wrinkles her brow, frowns, shakes his or her head slowly, and says those magic words, "I'll have to talk to my sales manager." Usually, there *is* no sales manager. The salesperson simply leaves you in the room to stew and sweat a little bit. You start second-guessing your last offer—and negotiating against yourself.

It's good practice never to go into a negotiation with unlimited authority to close the deal, even if everyone has given you preapproval to do so. Always have someone you must go back to for approval. If you *do* have ultimate authority, never let negotiators for the other side know it. Once they find out you are the sole decision-maker, they know you are the only obstacle in the way of the terms and conditions they want. There is just one person to convince.

> **Manager Alert**
> Never let negotiators for the other side know you are the sole decision-maker in a negotiation. If they find out you are, they'll know you are the only obstacle in the way of the terms and conditions they want.

The ambiguous authority tactic is usually employed just before the close of a negotiation. The other side thinks it has a deal, and all of a sudden there is someone else, or even a whole new cast of characters, to deal with. The last thing the other side wants is for this mysterious other person to blow a deal that is so close to being consummated. Negotiators may start to second-guess themselves and be tempted to soften their positions a bit to help you "sell" the deal to the other authority. They actually might start making additional concessions without demanding something in return. In effect, they start bidding against themselves.

Always try to keep your ambiguous authority as vague as possible. This prevents the other side from immediately countering your tactic. If you hold out your boss as your ambiguous authority, the other side may simply ask you to bring that person into the negotiation. It's harder for them to put a face on something vague like "the review committee," "my finance folks," or "my customers."

COUNTERS TO THE AMBIGUOUS AUTHORITY TACTIC

The best way to counter the ambiguous authority tactic is to head it off at the pass. Simply refuse to negotiate with anyone who doesn't have ultimate authority to bind the company. Remember, you control the process—including setting and running the agenda. When you send the other side a copy of your draft agenda for review, simply ask who the negotiator will be and if that individual will have ultimate decision authority. Get it in writing.

If the other side shows up with a different negotiator, establish the extent of that person's authority before the negotiation begins. If he or she doesn't have the final say, call off the negotiation until the other side can provide someone who does. Even if the originally designated negotiator shows up, always reconfirm that individual's authority before starting the negotiation. Always ask the question—and never negotiate with someone who can't make the final call and sign the agreement.

If you miss that chance and are confronted with an ambiguous authority, counter with an ambiguous authority of your own. You now also must run the "draft" deal by your own higher-ups for approval. Suddenly the other side is confronted with the possibility of your side changing the deal. If the other side's ambiguous authority is a tactic and it doesn't know whether yours is or not, it will usually back off.

Chapter 18

THE BRACKETING TACTIC

Bracketing is actually both a negotiation preparation tool and a tactic. When you prepared for the negotiation, you established a minimum position (MIN), target position (TGT), and maximum position (MAX) for each issue. Doing so built in negotiation flexibility and helped you set your BATNA—that crucial walk-away point. In essence, you bracketed your own objectives. Now we'll see how bracketing can be used as a tactic.

Since the other side will not willingly give away its MIN, MAX, and TGT positions, you need to bracket its offer. This will be easy if you remember that the first side to throw out a number in a negotiation usually loses. Put another way, *never* give out the first offer; *always* try to get the other side to make the first offer. As soon as one side throws out a number, you can create your bracket. That number becomes your MIN and you use it to establish a MAX and a TGT. You shift the entire negotiation range up before you even start negotiating in earnest.

> **Manager Alert**
> The first side to throw out a number in a negotiation usually loses. *Never* give out the first offer; *always* try to get the other side to make the first offer.

Government negotiators have the decided advantage in this tactic because the acquisition process forces the contractor to commit to the first number when it responds to a government solicitation. But the tactic of bracketing can apply to your first counterproposal as well. As soon as you counter the contractor's proposed price, its negotiators will bracket your counter. So make sure you do your homework and know the value of what you are buying. Also, never be predictable in your bracketing increments.

Here's another tip related to bracketing: Never offer to split the difference, but always encourage the other side to do so. When you split the difference, your side picks the number in between the two positions. That gives the other side a number it can bracket. It may then try to get you to split the difference again and again, constantly shifting the negotiation range upward.

COUNTERS TO THE BRACKETING TACTIC

The best counter is never to let the other side trick you into committing first. Never throw out the first number. If you don't give your number or position, the other side can't bracket it. If it tries to force you to commit, say "You're the expert—you tell me." Or "What do you think is fair?" Or "You tell me what your company needs to make a decent profit on this work." And remember, never offer to split the difference.

Next, always keep your government cost estimate secret. Never let the contractor find out how much you think the job will cost or how much you have planned to cover the acquisition. The only exception to this is construction contracts, where the FAR allows you to disclose an estimated price range to give competing contractors a ballpark for estimating the extent of the job.

Chapter 19

THE SET-ASIDE TACTIC

Deadlocks happen in negotiations, and the set-aside tactic is specifically designed to break deadlocks. Whenever the other side insists on a number or an issue that deadlocks the negotiation, simply acknowledge the contractor's position and suggest setting it aside for a while and moving on to other issues. Say something like, "I can tell this issue is important to you, and it's obvious we're pretty far apart on it. To keep the negotiation moving, let's set that issue aside for the moment and see if we can't get some of these other issues out of the way." If the other side is truly interested in reaching an agreement, it will always agree.

Then restart the momentum of the negotiation by getting agreement on many of the smaller (or noncontroversial) issues. This gets both sides into the swing of the give-and-take of the negotiation again. And the more you agree on issues, the more the other side will be under pressure to keep the ball rolling and continue to agree. After you have reconditioned the other side back into the habit of saying "yes," reintroduce your tabled issue. Chances are, the other side is now more willing to come to some agreement on it—to meet you more than halfway—to continue the momentum of the negotiation.

COUNTERS TO THE SET-ASIDE TACTIC

First, don't be too hasty to counter an offer at all. Setting aside the sticky issue may be just as healthy and appropriate for your side as it is for the contractor. You can also reverse the effects of the tactic by simply taking it over. If the other side proposes to set an issue aside, say something like, "Fine. Let's table this issue until later and see if we can get some agreement on all these other points. Let's have a caucus and I'll rearrange our agenda so we can get to these other issues."

Keep in mind the most powerful counter to the set-aside tactic: You are the government, so you control the agenda and the negotiation. Don't let the other side take away this powerful inherent advantage you enjoy. When a contractor pulls out the set-aside, you get to reset the agenda and now can order the revised agenda to encourage agreement on minor issues to build momentum and create time investment. You can literally hijack the other side's own tactic! Of course, you can also disagree to set aside the issue and continue the negotiation if you feel it is in your interest to do so.

> **Manager Alert**
> Controlling the agenda gives your side tremendous negotiating power.

Chapter 20

THE TRADEOFF TACTIC

The tradeoff tactic is always insisting on reciprocity for any concession. Simply, never make a concession without getting something in return: "If we do this for you, what will you do for us"? Never unilaterally throw them an unreciprocated concession as a gesture of goodwill. Never give them something for nothing.

Simply asking for something in return may get you something. By asking for a tradeoff concession, you also increase your negotiating capital. When you give up something without getting anything in return, you deplete your negotiating capital.

Negotiation capital is simply the cumulative negotiation latitude you have created in your plan. Don't deplete your "wiggle room" without at least attempting to get something in return. Doing so decreases your freedom to bargain and limits your other options, including which tactics you can employ. Always decide how much ground you can give up. Put a value, preferably a dollar value, on what you're willing to give up so you can ask the other side to reciprocate.

> **Manager Alert**
> By asking for a tradeoff concession, you increase your negotiating capital. When you give up something without getting anything in return, you deplete your negotiating capital.

By demanding a tradeoff, you also increase the cost to the other side for asking. Remember, you have already determined your position to be fair and reasonable. Let the other side know it will be difficult for you to agree to the concession, and you expect reciprocity to maintain fairness. If you always do this, it will make the other side less inclined to ask for "freebies" in the future. It will stop the other side from successfully using the nibble tactic on you.

COUNTERS TO THE TRADEOFF TACTIC

The tradeoff tactic is commonly used, so be prepared for it. Have preplanned answers to "If we do this for you, what will you do for us?" One counter could be to immediately offer one of your low priority "give" points. To do this, you must have already calculated what impact this will have on your overall negotiation plan

A more effective counter is to answer their question with a question. When they ask what you will do for them in return, ask "Well, what do you think would be fair?" In other words, let them suggest your tradeoff for you. Who knows, they may suggest you give up something that means little to you anyway.

Chapter 21

THE COUPLING TACTIC

In this tactic, you tie together, or "couple," certain of your "give" points with your "must" points, as if they're inseparable. You then present them to the other side as a package deal and negotiate them that way. You will argue long and hard for the "package" as if it is one important issue instead of an artificially constructed amalgam. When you finally relent and give up your "give" point, the other side usually reciprocates by giving you your "must" point.

Obviously, you want to couple issues that are compatible. Never attempt to couple totally dissimilar items; the other side will simply separate them back out and force you to negotiate them individually.

One "give" point that you can easily couple with almost any "must" point is price. Since you've already developed a MIN, TGT, and MAX position for each price issue, you already have price "give" points you can use. Couple all your "must" points to as many "give" points as you logically can.

COUNTERS TO THE COUPLING TACTIC

The best chance you have to counter the coupling tactic lies in your negotiation preparation. Identify common issues that the other side will likely attempt to couple. Likely candidates are price, delivery times, financing and warranties. The intel you have gathered prior to the negotiation should help you here.

You also have a natural counter to the coupling tactic simply because you are the government side. You control the agenda, so keep the initiative. Once you identify likely coupling targets, simply refuse to talk about them as packages. Set and control the agenda so all issues are treated and talked about separately.

> **Manager Alert**
> If the other side attempts to couple issues, simply refuse to talk about them as packages. Set and control the agenda so all issues are treated and talked about separately.

Your decoupling process may sound something like this: "I understand delivery time is an important issue to you, but we're talking about price right now. We'll cover delivery issues later this afternoon, I promise. In the meantime, why don't we stay on track with the agenda we both agreed to and finish our discussion on price? I know delivery time has an impact on your price, and we'll have time to discuss how all these issues affect each other after we get through talking about them individually." This forces the other side to talk individually about each and every point, both their "gives" and their "musts."

Chapter 22

THE EMPTY POCKETS TACTIC

The empty pockets tactic is simply confronting the other side with the fact that you have reached the limit of your negotiation flexibility, usually because you have run out of budget headroom. You say something like, "I really thought we could get this deal put together, but I simply don't have enough funds budgeted to allow me to sign this contract. I'd love to do it, but my pockets are empty."

Time is also something you can come up empty on. Your reason could be that funds are expiring or that your program office has deadlines it must meet. This puts pressure on the other side to concede within the money/time you have stipulated or risk losing the entire deal.

Before you decide to use this tactic, a few cautions are in order. First, remember you must be honest. As a government negotiator, you can't bluff or lie to the other side. If you say your pockets are empty, they must really be empty. Next, this tactic is best used at the end of a negotiation and even then only as a last resort. When you reveal to the other side that you have no more money in the budget or time in the schedule, you have automatically decreased your negotiation flexibility. You have given the other side important information about your position, possibly even your BATNA.

> **Manager Alert**
> As a government negotiator, you can't bluff or lie to the other side. If you say your pockets are empty, they must really be empty.

COUNTERING THE EMPTY POCKETS TACTICS

If the negotiators for the other side say they just don't have it in their budget, just don't have the time, or experience, or plant capacity, remember that's their problem, not yours! They are probably hoping you'll be sympathetic to their plight—but it's *their* plight. Resist the urge to feel sorry for them simply because they didn't budget or plan correctly. Don't fall for the guilt trip.

Contractors usually use the empty pockets tactic on modification requests after the basic contract has been negotiated and awarded. When you agreed to the basic contract, you agreed to a certain risk-sharing relationship between the government and the contractor. Part of that agreement represented the contractor's profit, which is largely a reward for risk taken. The contractor has already been compensated to assume the risk of not having enough of this or that. So if the scope of the contract remains unchanged, don't allow the empty pockets tactic to convince you it needs more of what it doesn't have or it needs to be compensated extra because it just didn't plan for enough.

Immediately probe an empty pockets assertion for validity. Is it really a deal-breaker or is the contractor just trying to get a leg up in the negotiation?

Chapter 23

THE CLIMATE CONTROL TACTIC

This is a manipulative tactic, so government negotiators shouldn't use it, but you had better know about it so you can counter it if it's used against you.

Prior to the negotiation, the other side makes the temperature in the room a little too hot or a little too cold on purpose. Not too noticeable, but a little uncomfortable. This imperceptibly pressures the victims of the tactic to come to some sort of agreement—even if it's not the best deal they could get—more quickly to get out of that uncomfortable situation as soon as possible. At the very least, you may become distracted by being too cold or too hot and lose some of your focus. The other side is already dressed appropriately so the tactic doesn't bother its negotiators.

COUNTERS TO THE CLIMATE CONTROL TACTIC

The government side controls the negotiation process, including the agenda and the venue, so the easiest counter is simply not to give up home court advantage. If at all possible, insist on having the negotiation at a facility you control. That puts you in charge of the thermostat. The only hand that should touch a thermostat in a negotiating room is yours.

If you can't control the venue, prepare your own team members. Tell them that since you don't know whether the room will be too hot or too cold, dress accordingly. Have them layer their clothes, so they can easily bundle up or shed off as appropriate. Dress coats and sweaters can easily be donned or taken off. Light jackets can be unobtrusively on hand.

Another simple counter is to request that the hosts adjust the room temperature. Train everyone on your team to come to you first privately if they are uncomfortable with the room temperature. You then approach the other side's leader and request the climate change in private. You may say something like, "We really appreciate the fine way you've prepared for us today. There's just one small thing. We believe it's too cold in here. I'm sure your folks are cold, too. Can you please bump the thermostat up at least three degrees? Once the room heats up a bit, we'll continue. We'd really appreciate it. You're all doing a great job, and thanks!"

Notice you use "we" instead of "I" and you make the problem a common one, mutual to both teams. Show that you won't be easily manipulated. Be specific in your request to make it more actionable and more difficult to be ignored or modified by the other side. You then signal that the negotiation will not continue until your request is met. You've done it nicely, but the message is clear. You then end with compliments and pleasantry. This improves the chances of having your request met without damaging your working relationship with the other side.

Chapter 24

THE STRENGTH-IN-NUMBERS TACTIC

This tactic taps into the fear of being outnumbered, even on a subconscious level, and is another one for government negotiators to watch out for but not to use. Manipulative negotiators know that simply outnumbering your team tilts the negotiation almost imperceptibly their way.

Of course, it's essential for negotiators to find out beforehand how many team members you will have so they can plan to have more. If they are the host, that's relatively easy. The host usually prepares a draft agenda and sends it out before the negotiation. In it, the host staff members will ask how many folks you plan to bring so they can make sure they have enough seats, refreshments, and so forth. What they really want is a nose count so they can have more people physically present in the room for the negotiation.

If the contractor is not the host, it will try to get a nose count of your team any way it can. The contractor may ask, for instance, what type of experts you'll be including (e.g., lawyers, program people) so it can make sure it has corresponding experts who can "talk the issues."

COUNTERS TO THE STRENGTH-IN-NUMBERS TACTIC

As with any tactic, the best way to counter the strength-in-numbers tactic is not to give it a chance to be used at all. Since you are the government side, you will usually be the host, so you'll control the agenda and the venue. You will send out the draft agenda. You also will select the room where the negotiation will take place, and you can use the physical seating limitations of the room (or your arrangement of it) to mandate the maximum number of folks the other side can bring. Simply state that the other side can bring no more than, say, five team members.

If the other side shows up with extra people, you can add team members of your own, if they are available. If they are not available, you can either elect to start the negotiation anyway or reschedule for when your additional players are available. You can say something like, "I see you brought your attorney and your VP for Sales. We weren't expecting that, or we would have made sure our lawyer's and program manager's schedules were clear for today. Just to make sure we can cover all the issues and truly get agreement from everyone at once, I'm going to reschedule our meeting for tomorrow, when our folks are available. That way, we'll be able to wrap this thing up in one session."

Chapter 25

THE WALK-IN-THE-WOODS TACTIC

This is another taboo tactic for you, but one to watch out for. It's normally pulled out well into the negotiation, after you've deadlocked on an issue or perhaps the entire negotiation has stalled. It's rarely recognized by untrained negotiators because it's disguised as a kind gesture, a great idea from the other side to break the deadlock.

After a long deadlock, the team leader for the other side will approach you and say something like, "You know, we're so close to getting this thing done, and we've been beating each other up on this one issue for the past two hours. My people are tired, and I know your folks are too. How about we put our teams on break, and we two get together somewhere—maybe the cafeteria for a cup of coffee, maybe outside for a breath of fresh air—and see if there's any way we can jointly work out some way to get this thing moving again." In essence, they ask you to take a walk in the woods. We know from fairy tales that nothing good ever happens in the woods.

You have now been separated from your entire support structure—and the team leader has it planned and you don't. You are isolated, unsupported, on unfamiliar ground, and at your weakest. Your counterpart already has a MIN, MAX, and TGT position and planned tactics to get you to agree with the contractor's way of resolving the deadlock. You are now at an extreme disadvantage.

The walk-in-the-woods tactic has a couple of lesser variations that are just as effective. One is for their team leader to pull you aside during a break or at lunch to discuss an "important issue" or a negotiating sticking point. Maybe he or she will offer to drive you to lunch. Again, you are isolated from your team.

Another variant is for certain members of the other team to do the same to their counterparts on your team. They'll pass it off as a "technical point that really only you and I are concerned about" or "something only the two of us are able to discuss technically." In reality, they're attempting to isolate your team members, either to gather more information or to convince them to come around to their way of seeing an issue.

COUNTERS TO THE WALK-IN-THE-WOODS TACTIC

Once you recognize the walk in the woods tactic, it's easy to counter—just stay out of the woods! Don't let yourself, under any circumstances, be isolated from your team by anyone from the other team. Your strength is in your team; absolutely refuse to be isolated from it. You may say something like, "That's a great idea to take a break. In fact, you read my mind. I was just about to call a caucus so I could go over how to overcome this deadlock with my folks. Let's go ahead and break for 15 minutes, then meet in our teams for the next, say, 30 minutes."

> **Manager Alert**
> Your strength is in your team; absolutely refuse to be isolated from it.

Surround yourself with your teammates during breaks; eat lunch with your team. Since any member of your team could become a victim to this tactic, familiarize them beforehand with the dangers of one-on-one discussions with the other side during breaks in the negotiation. Train them not to allow themselves to be isolated from the rest of the team. An added benefit could be improved team cohesiveness as you spend more time together, not just in the negotiation room but on breaks and at lunch as well.

Chapter 26

THE ANGER TACTIC

Anger is possibly the most powerful and volatile emotion we humans experience. Displays of raw anger bring out innate defensive mechanisms that are in themselves hard to control but usually give the angry person some benefit. Negotiators discovered this early in history, and feigned anger has been used as a tactic for a long, long time. To complicate matters, anger can be a purposeful tactic or it can be real.

Anger puts you on the defensive. Most people feel uncomfortable with conflict, and you might have a tendency to backpedal and give unilateral concessions. The members of the other side displaying their anger at you in front of your own team may be particularly effective. Now you have status, standing, and peer pressure to add to your worries. Worse, their anger can trigger your own anger in response. At the same time, it can increase the relative power of the negotiation position. They force you to see defusing their anger as one of your new negotiation objectives, one that you are willing to trade for a concession.

HANDLING ANGER

Anger is an extremely hard tactic to recognize; real or feigned, your response should be the same. If you're confronted by an angry negotiator, do not allow yourself to take it personally. Simply refuse to get personal and don't get angry back. Continue to treat the angry negotiator with courtesy. Control your own temper and hear him or her out. Resist the urge to retaliate, even if you have just cause to do so. Never interrupt an angry tirade. Don't confront the angry person on the issues as they are brought up, even if the facts are incorrect. Hear him or her out without defending your own position. Interrupting or trying to defend your position in the middle of a tirade will only further inflame anger. Admittedly, this takes practice!

As you listen patiently, take notes about what your angry opponent is saying, letting him or her see you taking notes. That shows you are listening and gives you a focal point to help you control your own anger and your impulse to retaliate.

Make sure to control the other members of your team and not let any of them interrupt or get angry either.

When the other person's anger is spent, calmly read back the essence of what was said. You may say, "So, I understand you are concerned about.... Do I have that correct?" That reaffirms that you have been listening. Notice that you *don't* say "I understand you are angry because...." I have personally found that angry people don't like to be told they are angry; that sometimes just bumps up their anger level a couple of notches. Don't try attempt to defuse anger with humor. Don't agree with his or her position—just let him or her know you understand the position.

After you have read back or restated the other side's position, give him or her a chance to respond. That not only makes sure you have the position correct, but it also gives the other side's negotiator another chance to blow off more steam (if there's any left). You want him or her deflated of as much anger as possible.

Next, call an immediate caucus or recess. That allows a cooling-off period; time defuses anger, for your side as well as the other side. A break additionally gives you and your team time to craft an appropriate, logically thought-out response. Finally, if the anger was really a tactic, it lets the other side know it won't be a fruitful tactic. It shows that the other side has been unsuccessful in pulling you into bad decision-making based on emotion rather than logic.

Here's one last point about handling an angry negotiator. You don't want his or her anger to stall the negotiation for any longer than is absolutely necessary for both sides to cool off and for you to craft a thoughtful response. Restart the negotiation as quickly as possible. As we've learned, time defuses anger. But if you let too much time pass unnecessarily, anger can reignite and grow even stronger. When you called a caucus, you promised the angry negotiator you would start back at a certain time. Make sure you honor that commitment. If you don't, the other side might think you are putting it off, are unconcerned with its issue, or worse, have no logical response to its position.

Chapter 27

THE PERSONAL ATTACK TACTIC

Personal attacks are rare, but you have to be ready to counter them if they are used against you. The other side may appear to be personally (and sometimes vocally) insulted by a position you've taken or something you've done. The contractor might criticize the quality of your work, your track record, or even your work ethic. The other side's negotiators might be personally discourteous to you by deliberately not making eye contact, showing up late for meetings, or interrupting you when you're talking. They might take cell phone calls or conduct other business in the middle of your negotiation session with them. If a trained negotiator resorts to personal insults, you can bet it's a tactic he or she is employing to gain a certain advantage.

Personal attacks used as a tactic are an attempt to break your concentration, throw you off balance, and make you feel uncomfortable. They are intended to get you to focus on yourself and your shortcomings instead of the issue being discussed. The other side is trying to make you feel less confident as a negotiator and as a person. Once sidetracked, you can't devote 100 percent of your mental ability to achieving your negotiation objectives. Personal attacks also partially shift your focus to rebuild or protect your ego instead of negotiating the best deal for the government.

HANDLING PERSONAL ATTACKS

If you are attacked personally, resist the urge to fight back. Work to put the negotiation back on an impersonal footing. Your simple refusal to react to the attack will dilute its intended purpose, preserve your relative power position, and signal to the other side that further personal attacks will bear no fruit.

> **Manager Alert**
> If you are attacked personally, resist the urge to fight back. Work to put the negotiation back on an impersonal footing.

In some cases, you can actually turn personal attacks into an advantage in the negotiation. If the other side claims it is personally insulted by your negotiation position, ask what it would consider not insulting. If the negotiator call you unfair, ask what would be considered fair. In both these cases, you're pulling a reversal on them—putting them on the spot to reveal more information about *their* negotiating position. This shifts negotiating power to your side. It also forces the other side to refocus on the impersonal issues of the negotiation.

If the personal attacks come in the form of discourteous behavior e.g., tardiness, inattentiveness, cell phone use let the person know the behavior is unacceptable but not in a confrontational or scolding way. You may say something like "Hey, listen. I know the world doesn't stop just because we're having this negotiation, but I was under the impression that this contract is as important to your company as it is to us. We have other demands too, and your [tardiness, inattentiveness, taking phone calls] is threatening to disrupt our other activities. Can we agree to focus on the issues at hand or should we reschedule this negotiation?"

Chapter 28

THE GUILT-TRIP TACTIC

Making the other side feel guilty about something is a common emotional tactic, even in government negotiations, simply because it works. When someone makes you feel guilty, it immediately works on your emotions. You often have an uncontrollable urge to cast off the guilt by "making it right" or somehow mollifying the "injured" party. The other side may try to make you feel guilty about something you have or have not done, a position you've taken, or any number of other things. These guilt trips are usually timed to come very close to the end of the negotiation.

The other side is hoping you'll respond emotionally to the guilt trip by softening your position or maybe throwing in an additional concession or two. It is hoping to hear the magic words "Well...just maybe we could...." The guilt-giver plays up the perception of your absolute dominance and control over the contractor's team members and their very livelihoods. From that lofty position, it's easier for you to throw a few more crumbs their way and not feel like you're giving up much of relative value. Besides, it alleviates your feeling of guilt. What a deal—for *them*!

COUNTERING THE GUILT-TRIP TACTIC

Just like anger and personal attacks, the best counter is to recognize that making you feel guilty is just a tactic and not let it affect you or lull you into unilateral concession giving. Test the validity of the other side's claim. The better you have prepared for the negotiation, the easier this will be, because you probably already have accumulated information to refute the claim. Are the negotiators really going to lose their jobs if you don't soften up? Is the company really going to fold if it doesn't get this deal? Do the negotiators really think you don't trust them?

The best way to test for validity is by probing with open-ended questions. For instance, you might respond with something like, "Did I hear you say your company may fold if you don't get this deal? How can a company that pulls in gross revenues of $626 million a year go bankrupt from losing just one contract?"

After you have recognized the guilt-trip tactic and tested it for validity, work to steer the negotiation back—as soon as possible—to focusing on the issues. You might say something like, "I understand you're personally concerned about that, but I don't see the bearing it has on coming to an agreement on the issues we're discussing. Let's concentrate on getting those resolved." Whatever response you use, make sure it separates the emotion from the issues and forces the discussion back to where it belongs—on the negotiation issues only.

> **Manager Alert**
> After you have recognized the guilt-trip tactic and tested it for validity, work to steer the negotiation back—as soon as possible—to focusing on the issues.

A final way to deal with a guilt attack is to reverse it. After the other side lays the guilt trip on you, ask, "If you were me, how would you respond to what you just said?" Or, "How do you think I should respond to your last comment?" This puts the negotiators on the spot, forcing *them* to confront what they're trying to make you do. If they're trying to make you feel guilty about a position you've taken on a particular issue, you might say, "Well, what do *you* think would be a fair solution?" In both cases, you've gone from defense to offense, forcing them to respond with a concession, an agreement to your terms, or, at the very least, additional information that could be useful to your side.

Chapter 29

THE FRUSTRATION TACTIC

A frustrated negotiator, whether genuinely frustrated or using frustration as a tactic, throws you off balance. If the negotiator gets so frustrated that he or she either walks out or mentally shuts down, he or she throws the entire weight of finding a solution onto your shoulders. The other side has set you up to negotiate against yourself.

Here's the problem. You can't simply stick with your own last offer because that's what frustrated the other side in the first place. If you offer an additional concession, the negotiators will have a legitimate excuse to reject it because they weren't involved in coming up with it.

Finally, the emotion displayed in becoming frustrated or exasperated has an emotional effect on you, too. The other side's negotiators want you to feel sorry for them because of all the pressures and deadlines they're under. You may be tempted to soften your position to make them feel better, show them you're a fair person, and get them back to the table. Under these circumstances, most negotiators will give up more than they planned and certainly more than they need to.

HANDLING FRUSTRATION

Don't let the other side's frustration stick you with both ends of the negotiation decisions. Whether it's feigned or real, identify it early and counter it. Interject yourself into the other side's bluster. Calmly and slowly tell the negotiators you understand and sympathize with the pressures they face. Your calm, measured tone will have a settling effect on the situation. Next, offer them a solution. Outline how they can beat their frustration by breaking the problem down into digestible chunks and focusing on the trees, not the forest. Also offer them the alternative of rescheduling the negotiation for a less chaotic time. If they are honestly frustrated, this may seem like a lifeline you've thrown them. If they are playing the frustration tactic, you have coolly negated its intended effects.

Don't attempt to solve the underlying problems that are purportedly causing the frustration. If you start working on those problems, even with the best of intentions, the other side may perceive that you've taken ownership of those problems. These problems are now magically your problems, not the other side's. Keep the other side in the game. Force it back into the give-and-take of the negotiation. Simply refuse to come up with a solution on your own without the other side's input. If that means rescheduling the negotiation, so be it.

> **Manager Alert**
> Don't attempt to solve the underlying problems that are frustrating your counterpart. He or she may perceive that you've taken ownership of those problems.

Your ultimate goal is to get the negotiation back on course as soon as possible. Calm the frustrated negotiator and sympathize with the position. Let him or her know he or she is not going to get away with tagging you and making you "it." Then reel the negotiator back into a discussion of the issues you need to resolve. Demonstrate that the only way the other side is going to get any result is to continue to negotiate.

Chapter 30

THE WALKOUT TACTIC

The walkout tactic is rarely used as a standalone tactic, but is often combined with other tactics such as the good cop/bad cop tactic and the anger tactic. Perhaps the most effective use of the walkout tactic is when it's combined with the frustration tactic. It is intended to shock, embarrass, and confuse your team. By walking out, the other side has created, out of thin air, another issue to use as a bargaining chip to gain concessions from you. Getting the other side's negotiators back to the negotiating table now becomes *your* problem and you'll feel pressure to throw them a bone—a unilateral concession—to have them sit down with you again. In effect, you start bidding against yourself.

COUNTERS TO THE WALKOUT TACTIC

When you're negotiating with experienced companies, you can rest assured that the walkout is a carefully calculated tactic being played by a professional negotiator. As you have learned, the best counter to any tactic is simply to recognize it as a tactic. That immediately takes most of the sting out of it. Look for telltale signs that the walkout is a tactic: Is the whole team leaving? (If not, you're being set up for the good cop/bad cop tactic.) Are they leaving something in the room, like a briefcase? Are they leaving before they have a ride back to the airport or way before their scheduled departure time? (If so, they're definitely planning to return.) Do they have competition for the contract? (If so, you can almost be assured it's a bluff.)

Let the other side know you recognize the dramatic walkout as a tactic. As soon as you see the negotiators start packing up or rising to head out the door, call their bluff. You might say something like, "Oh, come on Susan! You're not going to play the walkout tactic on me, are you? How about we take a 15-minute caucus instead and get back together and crunch this thing out? In fact, your team can stay in here and I'll take my team to the other room—I need to talk to them anyway about your last point. We'll be back in 15 minutes; is there any reason you won't be here then?"

This approach immediately lets the negotiators for the other side know that you recognize their actions as a tactic and that they won't be effective against you. You then immediately call a caucus to reassert control of the negotiation. If you allow the negotiators for the other side to walk out, you have ceded control to them. When you call a caucus, you signal to the other side that you don't consider the negotiation over—and that they had better remain engaged. But instead of challenging or demanding that they continue, you offer them the escape route of a caucus. That lets your counterpart save face in front of his or her team and greatly improves the likelihood that he or she will come back to the table.

> **Manager Alert**
> If your counterpart starts to walk out, offer the escape route of a caucus. Letting him or her save face in front of his or her team greatly improves the likelihood that the team leader will come back to the table.

Set a definite time to reconvene. This time is actually negotiable, and that's the point. If the negotiators for the other side start negotiating about the return time, they're still negotiating. And if they're still negotiating, they're still in the negotiation! Let them have any reasonable time they feel they need, but establish a definite return time before you allow them to leave. Maintain your control; don't cede it to them.

Chapter 31

THE LOCK-IN TACTIC

Lock-in tactics can be ultimatums or threats, actions the negotiators for the other side has already taken that they now want you to ratify after the fact, or actions they have taken that have intentionally restricted their negotiation room. They attempt to lock in positions, forcing you to concede for the negotiation to continue. There are several variants of this tactic.

THE CLASSIC LOCK-IN TACTIC

In the classic lock-in tactic, a negotiator will strengthen his or her bargaining position by intentionally weakening his or her own control over the situation. An example is when the other side's negotiator has vowed to upper management to get no less than a certain percentage increase from the government for the next year of contract performance. He or she intentionally attempts to set the negotiation range before the negotiation even starts.

The commitments are extreme, making it seem impossible for the other side to backtrack. You're almost put in the position of having to give a concession up front just to get the ball rolling. What's more, because the other side's negotiating position is so locked in, any concessions its negotiators do make will come at a high price to you.

THE FAIT ACCOMPLI

The fait accompli (French for "it is done") tactic relies on the saying "It's easier to beg for forgiveness than ask for permission." The negotiator for the other side assumes you'll agree to what they want to do beforehand, so they go ahead and do it before any agreement is reached. They then present you with the "fait accompli" and hope you'll simply accept it instead of going to the trouble of negotiating about it. Since the deed is already done, both sides are locked into the result.

TAKE IT OR LEAVE IT

Usually delivered near the close of a negotiation, this version of the lock-in tactic is designed to get you to commit, under pressure, to terms that are more favorable to the other side than to your side. The other side signals to you that it is perfectly willing to walk away from the deal (although usually that's the last thing it really wants to do).

Most experienced negotiators will use subtle phrases like "I'm sorry, company policy is that we never negotiate," "Sorry, but that's our walk-away price. We can't do it for anything less than that," or "We never deviate from our published prices." These are just softer forms of the "take-it-or-leave it" tactic.

Sometimes this tactic is used as a trick to get you to give away your entire negotiating range up front. The other side may say something like, "Just tell me how much you think it will take to get this deal done, and I'll let you know if we can do it for that amount." They are simply trying to get you to give them the first number so they can bracket it.

COUNTERS TO THE LOCK-IN TACTIC

Sometimes the hardest part is to divine whether the lock-in is being used as a tactic or whether it's a real bottom-line position. That's important, because you handle the two very differently. If the other side locks in because that's really all it has left to give, and if your side can't live with it, you're headed for a true, honest deadlock.

The best way to know the difference is to have done your homework. The more you know about the other side's position before you sit down to negotiate, the better able you are to determine if it is bluffing or not. If you suspect the other side is using the lock-in tactic, immediately test any data presented for validity. You may find it has reached its true bottom line. Or you could find that your facts contradict those of the other side and it is playing a tactic.

> **Manager Alert**
> The more you know about the other side's position before you sit down to negotiate, the better able you are to determine if it is bluffing or not.

Another effective counter to the lock-in tactic is to use the ambiguous authority tactic yourself to lock in your own position. You could say, "I understand you're saying you need at least $200 per hour, but I'm pretty sure my review committee won't go for it. I'm not even sure if it's in our budget. How do you suggest I sell them on the idea?" Not only have you used your own ambiguous authority to provide you a retreat route, but you've phrased it in a way that's almost certainly going to pull more information about the other side's position.

You could also try the trial balloon tactic, coupled with the "feel, felt" formula. It might go something like this: "I understand you feel you can't give any more on this issue, and I've felt the same way on a lot of issues I've negotiated. But what if we look at a longer delivery period? Could that have an effect on your pricing structure?"

Another nonthreatening approach could be to ask the other side what it would take to change its position. Either way, you're set to get more information and break the effect of the lock-in. You've shown you are flexible; if the negotiator for the other side doesn't reciprocate, they'll look inflexible.

Finally, you can counter the lock-in tactic by simply ignoring it. Blow it off as if you didn't even hear it. If you refuse to acknowledge it as a locked-in position, it doesn't lock you in. This puts the other side under more and more pressure to make good on the threat, and that's usually the last thing it wants to do. Most likely the other side will back down and modify its position if you simply let enough time pass without responding.

Chapter 32

THE DECOY TACTIC

In this tactic, the negotiators for the other side either make up a phony issue or forcefully press an issue they don't really care about to distract you from the real issue. In doing so, they are also creating a false issue they can later "give up," but only in return for a real concession from your side.

Since you represent the government, you cannot ethically use this tactic. You are required to be fair and reasonable to both sides, which means you can't make up imaginary issues to mislead the other side—simply put, you can't lie. Even though you can't use the decoy tactic, you have to be able to recognize it when it's used against you so you can counter it effectively.

> **Manager Alert**
> You are required to be fair and reasonable to both sides, which means you can't make up imaginary issues to mislead the other side—simply put, you can't lie.

COUNTERS TO THE DECOY TACTIC

The decoy tactic can be hard to recognize. By its very nature, it is designed to trick you into believing the other side's issue is important—when, in fact, it isn't. The better your market research is, the more you will know about the other side's goals—what's important to it and what isn't. The more you know about the other side's circumstances, the better you'll be able to judge whether it is genuinely concerned about an issue, is creating an issue out of thin air, or is puffing up a relatively trivial issue to wrangle a concession out of you that it really wants and couldn't get otherwise.

Once you recognize the decoy tactic, you have several options for countering it. The first is simply to ignore the decoy. Look for the underlying issue the other side is trying to decoy you away from and focus on that. Another option is to tackle the decoy issue head-on. Let the other side see you recognize the issue as legitimate and important—something you're willing to address. When you do this, you don't allow the other side an opportunity to unilaterally introduce a "fix" to the decoy issue that gives it what it really wants. Instead, you go on the offensive and take the initiative for fixing the decoy issue away from the other side.

As an alternative, instead of suggesting a solution to the decoy issue at this point, you may want to use the ambiguous authority tactic, deferring the decoy issue to your ambiguous authority. You can then follow it up with the good cop/bad cop tactic, putting the blame for not giving in on the decoy issue on the shoulders of your bad cop—who is also your ambiguous authority. Then offer an acceptable alternative to the decoy issue.

This combination of tactics isolates the decoy issue, turns it into a real issue (the very thing the other side doesn't want), and twists it to your advantage via the tradeoff tactic. You'll give on the decoy issue, but only if the other side gives on something in return.

Chapter 33

THE DELIBERATE MISTAKE TACTIC

You definitely cannot use this tactic. Because it involves deliberate deception, it is considered negotiating in bad faith; as a government negotiator, you can't negotiate in bad faith, lie to, or intentionally mislead a contractor in negotiations. However, you need to know how to spot the two versions of the deliberate mistake tactic—phony facts and deliberate omissions and errors—and understand how they work.

PHONY FACTS

This version of the deliberate mistake tactic occurs when the other side intentionally makes up or misrepresents facts, misrepresents its authority, or deliberately misstates its intentions. Negotiators for the other side lie and mislead you to gain an advantage in the negotiation. Contractors might say something like, "This is the lowest per-hour labor price we ever offer. It's the same and only price we always charge all our government clients." In reality, contractors could be deceiving you into accepting a high per-hour labor price that they have lowered for other government contracts in the past.

Or they might say something like, "I promise you we will keep our highest quality people dedicated to this effort." In reality, the contractor plans to pull these folks and replace them with their scrubs as soon as the contract is awarded.

Another example is a contractor intentionally submitting false charges or inflated numbers in a request for payment or a contract adjustment request. It will usually pick things that will be difficult or impossible for you to verify or are convoluted and complicated. The contractor is relying on your lack of knowledge or the sheer volume of work to scare you off from digging deep enough to uncover the truth.

The other side may also intentionally misrepresent the extent of its authority. It leads you to believe it has authority to finalize the deal, which gets you to reveal your bottom line. The contractor then claims it must defer to an ambiguous authority (think car salesmen here). Whatever excuse the other side comes up with, it's going to be extremely hard for you to prove deliberate deception.

Negotiators for the other side could also attempt to deceive you by making up phony "facts" to support their position or convince you to make decisions favorable to them. They could point to nonexistent or highly doctored surveys, engineering analyses, market research data, and the like. They could claim phony start-up costs, mobilization costs, or labor charges for work never done. They could claim acceptance of their product or service by certain regulatory groups or industry authorities that either don't exist or have never heard of them. There are hundreds of possible examples.

Finally, negotiators for the other side can deliberately misstate their intentions. They might say something like, "If we win this contract, I assure you it will be our company's absolute number one priority!" when they actually intend to relegate your contract to the back burner once award is clinched. True intentions are hard to prove up front, and the company can always argue that a changed situation forced it to back off its earlier assurances.

COUNTERING PHONY FACTS

The best way to counter phony facts is to know the real facts yourself. That comes from good negotiation planning backed up by thorough market research. Become an expert on what you're buying before launching into the negotiation, or use the expertise of other team members. You will then be able to challenge the other side's facts, figures, and assumptions if they appear to be phony. This will put negotiators for the other side on the defensive, needing to prove everything they say. They've lost their right to be dealt with by you in a trusted way.

Request background data or evidence to support any claims or assertions that seem questionable. Call a caucus and don't let the other side back into the negotiation without the documentation. Caucus again once you receive the documentation so your team can pore over and verify it without the pressure of being in the negotiation room with the other side. Take as long as necessary. Don't be rushed.

Once you determine that the other side has used "doctored" numbers or phony facts, you must respond quickly and decisively. Intentionally lying or misleading the government is not a healthy thing for anyone to do, and you represent the government. Point out the incorrect information and let the other side know that you know it's not valid. Offer the negotiators for the other side a chance to rethink their position or correct their mistake or to show you further evidence supporting their position, and refuse to continue the negotiation until they do. After they have revised their information, you then can resume the negotiation from that new perspective.

If it's absolutely clear that their phony facts are intentional, or if you have relied on deliberately phony facts to the detriment of the government, you may have to take advantage of the laws that protect the government. Be smart and engage the assistance of your legal counsel before proceeding. Here is a summary of some of your legal remedies:

1. *False Statements Act (18 U.S.C. 1001)*—Sets up criminal prohibitions against providing false statements to the government. Provides for fines and up to five years in jail.
2. *Possession of False Papers to Defraud United States (18 U.S.C. 1002)*—Makes it a criminal offense to knowingly and with intent defraud the government with any false, altered, forged, or counterfeited writing or documents.
3. *Major Fraud Against the United States (18 U.S.C. 1031)*—Makes it a criminal offense to knowingly execute or attempt to execute fraud against the government. Provides for fines up to $1 million dollars and up to 10 years in jail.
4. *False Claims Criminal Offense Statute (18 U.S.C. 287) and Civil Statute (31 U.S.C. 3729*, also known as the *False Claims Act)*—Provides for a civil penalty of not less than $5,000 and not more than $10,000, plus three times the amount of damage the false claim caused the government, per occurrence.
5. *Mail Fraud (18 U.S.C. 1341)* and *Wire Fraud (18 U.S.C. 1343)*—Criminal statutes that can be applied in addition to and in conjunction with all the other laws.
6. *Program Fraud Civil Remedies Act of 1986 (31 U.S.C. 3802)*—Sets administrative remedies for false claims and false statements. Also provides for administrative penalties of $5,000 per false claim or statement.
7. *Truth In Negotiations Act (10 U.S.C. 2306a and 41 U.S.C. 254a)*—Covers defective pricing on certain types of contracts.

In addition to criminal, civil, and administrative statutes, other actions can be taken against those who provide the government phony facts on purpose. These include voiding contracts, being placed on the excluded parties list, being determined nonresponsible for future contracts, and having a record of poor past performance in evaluations for future contracts.

Manager Alert

If it's absolutely clear that their phony facts are intentional, or if you have relied on deliberately phony facts to the detriment of the government, you may have to take advantage of the laws that protect the government. Be smart and engage the assistance of your legal counsel before proceeding.

DELIBERATE OMISSIONS AND ERRORS

The second version of the deliberate mistake tactic is the deliberate omission of material facts and the making of "accidental errors" that aren't really accidental at all. It occurs when the other side intentionally leaves out a fact that has a significant bearing on the negotiation. It also occurs when the negotiators for the other side knows you're thinking things are one way while they know for a fact they're not that way at all. Accidental errors are usually math mistakes made on purpose with the expectation that you won't scrutinize them and will accept the deal along with the math error skewed in the other side's favor.

Sometimes the other side knows you're incorrectly interpreting something either in your own requirements document or the proposal, and it will inform you of the correct interpretation only after the deal is sealed. It deliberately allows you to think your assumption or facts are correct by being silent and not correcting them.

Finally, the other side could intentionally commit errors in the proposal, hoping you won't catch them. Math errors in the other side's favor are the most common, although it can play with delivery dates, milestone dates, FOB points, discount terms, warranty provisions, levels of support, mean time between failures, mean time to repair, and the like. If you don't catch the "error," it could become part of the contract and then be legally binding on you.

COUNTERING DELIBERATE OMISSIONS AND ERRORS

Although this version of the deliberate mistake tactic is harder to catch than phony facts, your counter is essentially the same: Know your facts cold. The more you know about the situation, the more likely you are to spot key omissions and errors. When you do, let the other side know that the "carelessness" has caused you to seriously question the credibility and accuracy of everything it tells you. From that point on, request more backup or corroborating data on everything. Make the other side work and dig; make it regret being so "careless."

> ### Manager Alert
> Let the other side know that the "carelessness" has caused you to seriously question the credibility and accuracy of everything it tells you. From that point on, request more backup or corroborating data on everything. Make the other side work and dig; make it regret being so "careless."

Chapter 34

SETTING THE STAGE FOR THE NEGOTIATION

You're now ready to conduct the actual negotiation event. We'll go over how to open the negotiation, how to conduct it, what to do, and what to avoid. Finally, we'll address the all-important topic of how to successfully close the negotiation and document the result so you have an executable and complete agreement. We start with how to set the stage for a successful negotiation session.

Since you represent the government, the negotiation should usually take place at your facility, or a facility controlled by you and your team. Home court advantage gives you a huge edge. Because you are the host, however, you have the additional task of preparing for and facilitating the negotiation. Proper preparation of the negotiating environment—the room and area in which the negotiation will occur—can greatly influence the tone and even the outcome of the negotiation. You want to create an environment that's conducive to business-like discussions, doesn't overlook comfort, provides relative privacy and freedom from interruptions, and generally allows the negotiation to proceed in a smooth, orderly manner. This takes planning well before the negotiation event.

Proper preparation of the environment establishes your control of the environment. It allows you to prepare certain tactics you've chosen to use with the other side, and it diminishes the other side's ability to use certain tactics against you. A well-prepared negotiation environment sends a strong nonverbal signal that you are in control. It strengthens your authority and puts you in the superior power position before the negotiation even begins. You want this mental advantage.

> **Manager Alert**
> A well-prepared negotiation environment sends a strong nonverbal signal that you are in control. It strengthens your authority and puts you in the superior power position before the negotiation even begins. You want this mental advantage.

As you prepare the negotiation environment, you will need to
- Reserve the rooms
- Clear schedules
- Check availability of your extended negotiation team and supporting cast
- Set up the room
- Plan lunch and breaks.

RESERVE THE ROOMS

Don't negotiate at your desk if you can help it; the potential for distracting interruptions is too great. You'll need to locate and reserve a room, preferably in your building and near your desk, large enough to seat both teams comfortably. Most agencies have a process you must go through to reserve rooms, so start as early as possible. Make sure you block the reservation for more time than you think you need, and make sure you have exclusive use of the room for that entire time.

Remember to reserve a smaller conference room as well so one team or the other will have a secure, workable place to retreat to for private caucuses. Block this room for the entire time also.

CLEAR SCHEDULES

Well in advance of the negotiation event, make sure your schedule has nothing on it that would require disrupting the negotiation. A pop-in and pop-out negotiator appears confused and loses much negotiation power to the other side. Make sure your boss, your staff, and your coworkers know you're hands-off during this period. No "Gotta take this call," no "Gotta sign this now," no "Gotta see the boss about this or that." Make the negotiation the center of your known universe until it is successfully concluded. And make sure anyone who could possibly interrupt you knows that it is.

It's equally important to make sure all the members of your team do the same. Each and every member of your negotiation team must understand that they're

Chapter 34: Setting the Stage for the Negotiation   93

devoted to this task and this task alone until it's done. Personally ensure that their schedules are cleared for the entire anticipated time of the negotiation. Take the extra step of calling their bosses and confirming that their schedules are cleared. If their bosses don't support you on this, elevate the matter to your own boss. It's that important.

CHECK AVAILABILITY OF YOUR EXTENDED NEGOTIATION TEAM AND SUPPORTING CAST

The folks you take with you into the actual negotiation event are usually just part of your negotiation team. You also have bosses, review committee members, legal staff and program managers, who will impact the negotiation event. Make sure these folks will also be in place and accessible during the negotiation. If not, you may be forced to stall or possibly even postpone the event, which will diminish your credibility and power in the negotiation. With proper planning, you can reduce the likelihood of an absence bringing your negotiation to a standstill.

SET UP THE ROOM

After you've reserved the room, cleared your own and your team's schedules, and verified the availability of your supporting cast, you can now concentrate on setting up the negotiation room for an effective, professional event. Make sure to allow plenty of time before the other side is expected to arrive to set things up. Better yet, set up the room the day before so you can concentrate on those details that always seem to crop up right before the other side arrives.

Use the schedule and logistics section of your negotiation plan (discussed in Chapter 5) for a useful list of items to prepare. You can come up with your own negotiation preparation checklist or use one your agency or office has standardized

Survey the room and arrange your team's seating for maximum effect. If possible, make sure your team is seated facing the door. That way, every member can see and control who goes in and out, as well as who may be trying to interrupt the negotiation.

Chapter 7 introduced you to the roles of team leader, good cop, bad cop, technocrat, and sweeper. Ideally, you'll have just one person playing each role. Seat them strategically around the table, preferably in an arrangement something like this:

Sweeper	Good Cop	Team Leader	Technocrat	Bad Cop
Negotiation Table				

The team leader should always be seated at the center of the table, in the middle of the team. This not only reinforces his or her authority and position, but lets him or her better control the activities of the team and interact with all members of the other side more easily.

The technocrat should be immediately next to the team leader (on either side). The technocrat is an excellent complement, backup, and reinforcement to the team leader, lending statistical and data support. Being next to the team leader also allows the technocrat to easily and subtly restrain a team leader who slips out of the negotiating range the facts and figures support.

The bad cop is placed next to the technocrat at the end of the negotiation table, preferably the end that is closest to the door. Since the bad cop's role often complements the role of the technocrat, this puts them in the ideal positions to play off each other. It also separates the bad cop physically from the team leader, allowing the team leader to maintain the perception of fairness and impartiality in the other side's eyes. Being next to the door enables the bad cop to storm out of the room easily if he or she is employing the walkout tactic, without tripping over cords, chairs, briefcases, or other team members.

The good cop is seated next to the team leader on the opposite side of the technocrat. This placement close to the center of the table allows the other side to focus on him or her as the good copy plays the role and endears himself or herself to the other side. Right at the team leader's elbow, the good cop can also be an affable "yes-person" to the team leader, wholeheartedly and pleasantly agreeing with important points the team leader makes.

The good cop's pleasant nature and willingness to agree with the other side's team members reinforces the team leader's role as a strong and resolute force. Physically separating the bad cop from the good cop also greatly enhances the effect of the good cop/bad cop tactic.

The sweeper is at the far end of the table next to the good cop. This allows him or her to observe everything that's going on in the room, and especially to pick up on hidden gestures or unusual actions by the other side. The sweeper literally has a "sweeping" panoramic view of the negotiation table.

It's a good idea to make nametags and place them where you want your team members to sit, so those places won't be taken by folks from the other side. If you know the identity of all the other side's team members (you should have asked for that information when you sent out the draft agenda), make nametags for them too. Before the other team arrives, assign seats simply by placing the nametags. This will reduce the chance the other side's team members will be able to play their own strategic seating game on you.

> **Manager Alert**
> Before the other team members arrive, assign their seats by placing the nametags you have made for them. This will reduce the chance they will be able to play their own strategic seating game on you.

PLAN LUNCH AND BREAKS

You probably have already set the times for lunch and planned breaks in your written agenda. Although it may seem trivial, a lack of planning exactly how and where you conduct these breaks could, at a minimum, disrupt the flow of the negotiation. Worst case, it could jeopardize a successful negotiation outcome for your team.

It's not advisable for you to go out to lunch with the other side. You need that time with your own team to review facts or pull thoughts together to be better prepared to continue the negotiation after lunch. You also need a mental break from the stress of the negotiation; it's hard not to continue to talk the issues if the other side's players are there. You also want to ensure that the other side can't corral one or two of your team members away from the rest of your group in an attempt to divide and conquer.

Bottom line, make plans to keep your team together during lunch and breaks. Plan for privacy. Have your own "retreat room" already set up for breaks and have your lunch venue planned in advance. You can provide the other side with a list of recommended restaurants, along with directions, when you send out your draft agenda. Let the negotiators for the other side take care of themselves—they probably want to use that time privately anyway. Keep your team together and focused on the negotiation. Having preplanned team lunches also prevents your team members from scurrying back to their offices to check emails, do other work, and get distracted from the negotiation.

Chapter 35

OPENING THE NEGOTIATION

Opening a negotiation properly involves eight steps:

1. Introduce yourself and your team.
2. Let the negotiators for the other side introduce themselves.
3. Establish your authority.
4. Verify the other side's authority.
5. Make an opening statement.
6. Allow the other side to make an opening statement.
7. Transition into your first tactic.
8. Throughout the previous seven steps, *listen*!

MAKE INTRODUCTIONS

If you are the government team leader, start the negotiation by thanking the other side for coming and by introducing yourself. Be timely about this, so you don't give the other side's team leader an opportunity to take control of the negotiation before it starts. You want to be firmly in control; it's *your* negotiation. Then introduce the members of your team by name and position. Do this even if you think the other side already knows them. Don't have your team members introduce themselves— do it for them. After all you team members are introduced, let the other side's team leader do the same for his or her team. Although the introductions themselves are a mere formality, they are your first chance to assert control over the negotiation and demonstrate your authority and ability to lead and control.

ESTABLISH YOUR AUTHORITY

After introductions are completed, establish your authority as the government team leader. Let the other side know that you are the team leader and as such are solely responsible for the conduct and flow of the negotiation. You will be calling breaks, setting lunch, calling quit times, and the like. Everything discussed in the session must go through and be approved by you.

Establishing your authority lessens the chance the other side will be tempted to try to divide and conquer or to take control of the flow of the negotiation. Don't be crass or domineering, just assured and in control.

VERIFY THE OTHER SIDE'S AUTHORITY

Make one last check on the actual authority of the other side's team leader to obligate his or her company without outside approvals or reviews. You should already have done this in your draft agenda process, but always verify right before you start negotiating. Don't ever start negotiating and revealing your positions until you verify the other side's authority to commit. You want to make sure you're dealing with only those folks at the table, not others who are not present. If you don't, the other side will be able to use the ambiguous authority tactic on you.

> **Manager Alert**
> Don't ever start negotiating and revealing your positions until you verify the other side's authority to commit. You want to make sure you're dealing with only those folks at the table, not others who are not present.

The best way to verify authority is to be straightforward: Just ask. The conversation could go something like, "Ms. Hester, before we start, I just want to make sure you have authority to commit your company to any agreement we may reach. I know that in your response to our draft agenda you said you have no boss, board of directors, or review committee you have to defer to. Is that still the case?"

If the answer to that question is no, seriously consider suspending the negotiation until the other side can provide someone able to commit its company. If you previously got the other side's promise, through their response to the draft agenda, to send someone with the required authority, this will undoubtedly be embarrassing to the other side. You have a defensible position to suspend the negotiation, and the other side will lose power when the negotiation resumes.

MAKE AN OPENING STATEMENT

Your opening statement should be a concise summary of why everyone is here. It should be very positive, delivered in a way that assumes that everyone is in complete accord with the general problem to be solved and will reach an amicable agreement on how to solve it. In fact, your opening statement could be in the form of a question like, "Folks, can we all agree we're here to find a better way to provide logistics support for our troops overseas?" (Wait for nods—that's something everyone should be willing to agree to.) "And can we all agree we need to find the fairest, most equitable solution that represents best value for all involved?" (Wait for more nods.)

Your opening statement unites both parties in a common cause and points everyone toward a common goal. It fosters trust and reinforces the idea that you are all, ultimately, on the same side. Never go into particulars or positions in your opening statement—focus on the ends, not the means.

> **Manager Alert**
> Never go into particulars or positions in your opening statement—focus on the ends, not the means.

ALLOW THE OTHER SIDE TO MAKE AN OPENING STATEMENT

After your opening statement, give the other side's team leader an opportunity to make his or her own opening statement. Other than just simply being courteous, this serves two purposes. First, you get verbal buy-in from the other side about the ultimate goal of the negotiation. The other side will rarely disagree with the ideas and goals you have presented in your opening statement since you couched them in such general terms. Its opening statement is usually a confirmation of the objectives and goals you have laid out. Once committed, the other side will have a hard time retreating from its commitment to finding an equitable, fair, and reasonable outcome along the general lines you have proposed. During deadlocks that may occur later, you can always remind the other team of its commitment.

Finally, the other side's opening statement could give you important clues and key information about its plans, strategies, tactics, and goals for the negotiation. It could also give you a sneak peek into what you can expect from it. If the other side agrees with your opening statement in general but voice some reservations about your ambitious delivery dates, for instance, you now have additional key information about what's important to it. This allows you to adjust your strategy and tactics accordingly.

TRANSITION INTO YOUR FIRST TACTIC

Here's where you start executing your negotiation plan. There's no set way to go here; it will depend on the situation and what you have set up in your negotiation plan. Remember, you already have the other side's proposal and you've had time to evaluate it. Negotiators for the other side will be expecting you to start by giving them some feedback or reaction to what they have already given you. Nevertheless, you can transition into the negotiation by stating no position, stating your MIN (best case) position, stating your TGT position, or attacking their proposed position.

I am a big fan of starting off by stating no position. You may begin with something like, "We've read your proposal and we think we understand it." Then ask a question like, "Have you had any further thoughts on what you've sent us?" "Has your thinking changed on anything?" "Has anything new come up we should know about before we start?" These types of open-ended questions immediately put the negotiators for the other side on the defensive and tend to pull them into elaborating on their proposal. You don't tell them you think their proposal is good or bad; you just ask them about it in general. You may even be able to get concessions from the other side without giving up a single thing—and the negotiation has just started!

You could also start off by revealing your MIN (best case) position and gauging the other side's reaction to it. If you have determined that your side has a lot of relative power in the negotiation, this is another effective way to start. If you perceive your relative power to be somewhat weaker than the other side's, you may want to start off by revealing your TGT position. That could lead to a quicker agreement, but it does rob you of some negotiation headroom.

The last way to transition into the negotiation from your introduction is to start addressing, point by point, weaknesses or other issues you are concerned about in the other side's proposal. Be very careful with this approach; it immediately engenders an "us versus them" mentality, throwing the other side into a defensive crouch and unraveling much of the goodwill you created in your opening statement. Eventually, some of these hard issues will have to be addressed, but there's generally no need to hit the other side in the face with them from the get-go.

LISTEN!

The very start of the negotiation is the most crucial time to pick up useful information about the other side's real agenda and positions. Negotiators are most unguarded at this point, especially if you have done a good job setting the stage with an effective opening statement. Keep attuned to everything they say, how they say it, their mannerisms, their body language, their reactions to your statements, and their responses.

This is the first time you may be able to figure out who, for instance, is going to be the other side's bad cop, which tactic it has decided to start off with, or what's truly most important to the other side. Be all ears—and have your team members be all ears.

Chapter 36

CONDUCTING THE NEGOTIATION

After you have opened the negotiation and transitioned into your first tactic, conducting the negotiation should be a simple matter of following your negotiation plan. Your plan, however, has to be flexible enough to incorporate inevitable changes as the ebb and flow of the negotiation progresses. Here is a list of negotiation "Dos" and "Don'ts" you can use as a guide.

DO'S

- Know your authority as a negotiator and that of your counterpart.
- Have respect for the other side's position and viewpoints.
- Keep the overall objectives of the negotiation clearly in mind.
- Be fair and reasonable to both parties.
- Obtain and maintain the initiative.
- Establish an ambiguous authority.
- Get the other side to commit first. (It enables bracketing.)
- Prepare a memorandum of what happened after each negotiation session. Prepare interim summaries as agreements are reached on individual issues immediately after agreement.
- Remember you're not in the negotiation alone. Use your team of experts to help you prepare for and conduct the negotiation.
- Be unpredictable. Mix up your strategies and tactics so you don't use the same ones all the time.
- Be patient. Generally, 80 percent of concessions come in the last 20 percent of the negotiation.

- Tailor your negotiation for each offeror in the competitive range. Evaluate their offer against the solicitation not other offerors' proposals.
- Realize that FAR Part 15 does not require you to reach agreement on every element of cost. Stick to the major issues and the cost drivers.
- Know the difference between "cost" and "price" (price = cost + profit or fee).
- Use a contract type that allocates risk fairly. Remember, contract type is usually negotiable.
- Understand how to interpret body language.
- Carefully guard your travel schedule (or keep your return date open).
- Always ask open-ended questions. Questions phrased so they can be answered by "yes" or "no" give you limited information.
- Practice active listening. Use summary phrases such as "Did I hear you correctly in saying…?" or "From what I'm hearing you tell me, your point is…."
- Even though you have someone to take official minutes, let the other side see you taking notes.
- Redirect personal attacks on you as attacks on the problem.
- Pause after asking a question; don't be a motor mouth.
- Ask for more than you expect to get; it gives you negotiating room.
- Start with a high initial position if you don't know much about the other side.
- Flinch at the other side's proposals. React with visible shock and surprise. A concession often follows a flinch.
- Position the other side to feel good about the negotiation by making a small concession at the end.
- Consider "no" as simply the other side's going-in position.
- Position your most difficult issues last. The more time you can get the other side to invest, the more likely you are to get concessions as the negotiation drags on.
- Control the pace of the negotiation.
- Make sure when you give on your "give" points, it brings you closer to agreement on your "must" points. Control the order of issues to make this happen.
- Feel free to call a caucus anytime you are confused, lose control of your team, or need to reevaluate.
- Use the tactics outlined in this book, if it's fair for you to use them.
- Watch out for the tactics outlined in this book and be prepared to counter them.

- Feel free to use and be on the lookout for any other tactics not covered in this book—there are hundreds of tactics!

DON'TS:

- Never reveal or discuss your position, strategy, or tactics to anyone besides those who absolutely need to know.
- Don't give up big chunks of negotiating room up front.
- Don't make concessions without getting something in return. Ask for one right away.
- Don't try to become well liked or popular with the other side during a negotiation.
- Never allow more than one person on your team to talk at once on a given issue.
- Never allow your team to be separated, even during breaks or lunch.
- Never let the other side witness disagreements among your team members (unless it's planned).
- Never bluff unless you are willing to have your bluff called.
- Never sign an agreement you don't consider fair and reasonable.
- Never negotiate unprepared.
- Never engage in conduct that
  - Favors one offeror over another
  - Reveals an offeror's technical solution to another offeror
  - Reveals an offeror's price without its permission
  - Reveals sources of past performance data
  - Knowingly furnishes source selection information in violation of the Procurement Integrity Act.
- Never indicate to offerors that they will win the award.
- Don't make up false statements or cite fictitious regulations.
- Don't allow contractor "buy-in."
- Don't allow an offeror's low initial price to overshadow lifecycle cost considerations.
- Avoid entanglement in personal issues. Don't take the negotiations personally.
- Don't react to emotional outbursts. Let the other party blow off steam.
- Don't go in with your best offer up front. It leaves no room for the other side to feel it has successfully negotiated and won.
- Never say yes to the first offer or counteroffer.

- Never offer to split the difference. Encourage the other side to offer to do it. You don't have to split down the middle. You can use its willingness to get closer to your objectives. You can split more than once.
- Don't make your last concession a big one. Doing so could create hostility.
- Avoid making equal-sized concessions. This will encourage the other side to keep pushing.
- Don't let the other side write the contract, write the memorandum of agreement, or take the official minutes.
- Don't be afraid to admit you don't know and to ask questions.
- Don't narrow the negotiation down to one issue. If you do, you will have to have a clear winner and a clear loser.
- Don't assume the other side wants what you want.

Chapter 37

CLOSING THE NEGOTIATION

How you close the negotiation is just as important as how you start the negotiation. As the leader of the government team, it's your responsibility to lead both sides toward closure, signaling when it's time to close and document the results. You've got to be good at closing, or the negotiation could wander interminably. The longer it does, the more opportunity there is for additional problems to crop up, situations to change, and conflicts to arise over minor issues.

Salespeople of all stripes are taught to look for "closing signals" from the other side. Certain body language, phrases, or activities can be clear indicators that the other side is ready to close. Since you are usually the buyer, not the seller, you have control over when the close occurs and how it will happen. You will need to prepare to execute the close, make sure everyone is truly in agreement, and make everyone feel like a winner.

PREPARING TO CLOSE

When you're ready to close, instruct your team privately that you will be doing all the talking from this point on. When you take over all communication for your team, it's a clear signal to the other side that you're moving to close. It focuses all the attention on you without the possibility of getting sidetracked. Start drawing together, in big-picture terms, all the agreements you have reached on all the issues discussed. Ask the other side if it agrees with your summary—you want the other side to commit to your view of how things stand. If you don't, loose ends or disagreements may unravel everything you've done. Start talking about end-game terms such as method and frequency of payment, delivery terms, and warranties. As you do this, let your body language also signal that you're ready to close.

> **Manager Alert**
> When you take over all communication for your team, it's a clear signal to the other side that you're moving to close. It focuses all the attention on you without the possibility of getting sidetracked.

WAYS TO CLOSE

The following sections highlight a few of the most common ways a government negotiator can choose to close. Most of the principles are borrowed from commercial sales training, modified for the unique situation of a government negotiator.

You'll have to gauge for yourself which one of these six methods of closing is right for your particular situation. You may like other closing methods that work well for you; if you do, use them. These closing methods can also sometimes be used together for better effect, either sequentially or in combination.

Total Agreement Close

The total agreement close is the most common and best way to close. It simply involves summarizing and agreeing in total to all the individual issues you have discussed and agreed to so far. Through the give-and-take of the negotiation, both sides have made concessions that have been agreeable to all. You may have wanted more on this issue, the other side may have wanted more on that issue, but you all can agree on the total package.

Emphasize the benefits to both sides of accepting the agreement as a whole. Assure the other side that agreeing on the total package won't set precedents for future negotiations on individual areas it might not be too happy about. Use this close when you have been able to reach agreement on all of the important issues and most or all of the lesser issues.

Ambiguous Authority Close

Use the ambiguous authority close if you still have unresolved issues that you do not want (or have no more room) to move on, but closing the negotiation now is in the best interest of the government. First, summarize all the points of agreement. Then inform the negotiators for the other side of your final position on the contentious issues and tell them you have no authority to move more, blaming your lack of flexibility on your ambiguous authority. Of course, you would have had to set up an ambiguous authority beforehand to use this close.

The ambiguous authority close may go something like, "I've made the best argument I could, but the review committee has given me no authority to make any other offer." "Sorry, folks, but this has to be my final offer. My supervisor absolutely refuses to make any more funds available over what I have right now." "I tried my best to present your argument to the Director, but she's adamant that if we can't agree to the terms and prices on the table now, she'll look for another alternative to meet our need."

This close is intended to force the other side to accept your position as it stands—or risk getting nothing. The danger, of course, is that the other side might just choose to accept nothing rather than go through with the deal. You should have already protected yourself against that possibility by establishing your BATNA.

Power Close

The power close assumes that the other side needs the deal more than you do. Avoid using the power close unless absolutely necessary, as it could be viewed as intimidation.

The power close is essentially the ambiguous authority close without the ambiguous authority. You present your final offer—take it or leave it. You're the government representative and you have determined that no other deal will be fair and reasonable.

You can elect to justify your position (e.g., lack of funds, cheaper alternatives) or you can simply lay it on the table without justification. You basically challenge the other side to fish or cut bait. Since the other side may choose to cut bait, you had better make absolutely sure you can live with your BATNA before you try this close.

> **Manager Alert**
> Avoid using the power close unless absolutely necessary, as it could be viewed as intimidation.

Either/or Close

With the either/or close, you give the other side a choice between two acceptable alternatives. Both alternatives must be acceptable to both sides. This close is best used when you have reached agreement on everything but one major issue and you have some tradeoff flexibility on that issue.

An either/or close could go something like, "Well, we're down to this. Either you agree to cut your price down to $50,000 if you can't meet our delivery date requirement or we'll pay you your total asking price of $75,000 if you meet the delivery date. The choice is yours." The alternatives don't have to be equally acceptable, but you have to anticipate that both will at least be acceptable to the other side. Also, you've got to be willing to live with either choice yourself, since you've passed decision authority for choosing between them to the other side.

Silent Close

The silent close is commonly used by salespeople. You perform it the exact same way you perform the silence tactic. You simply present the other side with your final offer and shut up. Be absolutely silent. The other side just may say yes. If it doesn't, your silence will soon get deafening, forcing the other side to give in and close or to throw in an additional concession to close.

Split-the-Difference Close

Splitting the difference is a common way many negotiations, government and otherwise, end up being concluded. This close is used when both sides have agreed on everything else but that all-important issue: price. You're down here and the other side is up there, and that difference is the only thing holding agreement back. At this point, many, many government negotiators make the mistake of offering to split the difference 50/50 to reach an agreement—but that's not the split-the-difference close! You know that you should never offer to split the difference. The split-the-difference tactic encourages the other side to split the difference.

> **Manager Alert**
>
> You should never offer to split the difference. The split-the-difference tactic encourages the other side to split the difference.

ENSURING TOTAL AGREEMENT

Whatever method of closing you use, you must make sure that both sides fully understand the terms and conditions they are agreeing on. At this point, you should not only confirm agreement on the total package but also make sure that all sides see the details the same way. Take a look at the terminology you're using, define the terms clearly, and ensure agreement on the definitions. Remember, ambiguities are construed against the drafter of the language, and this is your last chance to eliminate them.

Look at the details. What, exactly does "ASAP" mean? What do you mean by "within two weeks"? Two weeks from what? What exactly do you mean by requesting that the contractor "fully cooperate with the program office"? What's "fully"? What's "cooperation"? If differences in interpretation or misunderstandings arise up during this review, make sure they are addressed and agreed to—not left open-ended.

Lay out the terms in writing and have the negotiators for the other side look over them and agree to them. Have them sign the agreement and give them a copy. This doesn't have to be your official documentation of what went on in the negotiation, but it should be clear and complete enough to make sure the other side fully understands and agrees to the entire deal. If you have been keeping good notes and preparing interim summaries as the negotiation progressed, this should be very easy to do. Most of the work has already been done.

Finally, you can never close a negotiation knowing there's a mistake in the other side's understanding of the agreement, reasoning, expectations, facts, or figures. As a government negotiator, you must be fair and reasonable to all sides. If you know the other side has an erroneous understanding of the scope of its commitments, or a math error makes the price unreasonably low, you must disclose this.

> **Manager Alert**
> As a government negotiator, you must be fair and reasonable to all sides. If you know the other side has an erroneous understanding of the scope of their commitments, or a math error makes the price unreasonably low, you must disclose this.

MAKING EVERYONE FEEL LIKE A WINNER

Your job as a government negotiator is not to beat down the other side and "win" the negotiation. Your job is to negotiate a fair and reasonable agreement for both sides (and the taxpayer) that satisfies your mission requirements. A negotiation should never end with a "winner" or a "loser." Even if you have maxed out all your negotiation objectives, you should never feel smug or superior. Both sides need to win. This preserves the working relationship of the parties during contract performance and for any future negotiations.

Making everyone feel like a winner ensures that the final deal, be it a contract or a modification, will be carried out cheerfully and produce the results it's intended to produce. Always keep in mind that the ultimate goal of an acquisition is not contract award but contract performance. Whatever deal is eventually agreed to will now have to be carried out by the parties. If you have made the other side feel like a loser in the negotiation, its performance of the agreement may reflect resentment.

> **Manager Alert**
> Always keep in mind that the ultimate goal of an acquisition is not contract award but contract performance.

To make sure the other side feels like a winner too, save a little concession to give away at the end of the negotiation. It doesn't have to be a big concession—it's the thought that counts. Even if the other side views the concession as insignificant, it at least gives the other side the satisfaction of having the last victory in the negotiation. Make sure to make the concession at the very end of the negotiation so the other side will know it isn't expected to reciprocate. Doing this allows the other side to save face, make a positive showing to its bosses, and generally feel better about the deal. The cost of a small concession given in this way can return huge dividends in contract performance.

Next, make sure to congratulate the other side for a job well done. It doesn't matter how well the negotiators for the other side actually performed; congratulate them. Praise them for their professionalism and their negotiation skills. Tell them you learned something from them. They probably spent long hours preparing for the event just like you did, so let them know their time investment was productive. Everyone likes to have their self-esteem boosted and their value as an employee and an individual confirmed. Make them go away feeling good not only about the deal but also about you and about themselves. Win/Win is not always the best strategy to follow, but it should always be the perceived negotiation outcome.

> **Manager Alert**
> Make sure to congratulate the other side for a job well done.

Chapter 38

DOCUMENTING THE NEGOTIATION

As the saying goes, nothing is done in government work until all the paperwork is done. The next, and final, job of the negotiation process is to document the results. Both sides will perform not as agreed to in the negotiation but as documented in the agreement instrument. You will not administer the agreement by what you intended it to say but by what it does say. If disagreements, disputes, or protests later arise over your actions, what you intended will not matter much; what you documented will rule. That's how the courts and boards determine your intent.

> **Manager Alert**
> Both sides will perform not as agreed to in the negotiation but as documented in the agreement instrument.

If you kept good minutes, prepared written interim summaries, and did a good job of summarizing the final results of the negotiation immediately after it concluded, your job will be a whole lot easier. In addition, the results will be much more accurate, enforceable, and defensible. You should already have folded your interim summaries into your final negotiation summary, and you should already have reached agreement with the other side on your final negotiation summary. In a competitive negotiation, you should already have done this for each offeror you negotiated with. These pieces can now be welded together to paint a picture of the entire negotiation. In a sole-source negotiation, or if you are negotiating a modification or taking some other sole-source action, this final negotiation summary can become the primary source for your documentation actions.

THE PRICE NEGOTIATION MEMORANDUM

One of the things a government contracting officer must determine, before going into any agreement (e.g., contract, contract modification) that will obligate federal funds, is that the agreement is being entered into at a fair and reasonable price. In most cases this determination has to be backed up by some kind of written justification. For contract award decisions, that justification is usually called a price negotiation memorandum or PNM. This is the record of your negotiation and how you have determined the final outcome to be fair and reasonable. (If you are documenting a sole-source negotiation or a modification, it may be called a price justification or justification of fair and reasonable price. Check your agency's guidance.)

Remember, your final negotiation summary is not your PNM or price justification. The final negotiation summary is a record of what went on during the negotiation with a particular contractor and can be given to that contractor at the conclusion of the negotiation. Your PNM or price justification documentation contains *all* the information you considered to make your award decision or to determine the final price to be fair and reasonable. It will contain much more information than the final negotiation summary. Some of this information may still be procurement-sensitive or source selection information, so your PNM is never shared with the other side.

Different agencies vary widely on content, format, and dollar triggers for written PNMs and justifications, so you'll have to check your agency's guidance on how, what, and when to write. Usually this guidance can be found in your agency's supplement to FAR Part 15.

OBTAINING A RELEASE OF CLAIMS

If you have negotiated a modification to an existing contract, you may be required (or elect) to obtain a release of clams from the contractor. A release of claims is not required for contract award or for most contract modifications. It is required only for bilateral modifications that definitize negotiated settlements resulting from change orders issued against noncommercial contracts (see FAR Part 43.2). However, check your agency policy on when a release of claims is required. Your agency may want you to obtain a release of claims for other types of modifications in addition to what's required by the FAR.

Even if you're not required to obtain a release of claims by the FAR or by your agency's regulations, it's still sometimes a good idea to do so. The release of claims locks down the agreement so the contractor can't come back later and ask for additional adjustments as a result of a change. It also gives you extra security that the deal you struck for the modification is the deal the contractor will live with and that the compensation offered is all it will ask for.

OBTAINING REQUIRED REVIEWS AND APPROVALS

After you have prepared your documentation of the results of the negotiation, you *still* may not be quite done. Your agency may require some reviews and approvals before you can move to formalize the actual agreement. Check your agency's requirements, because each agency has different ones. Most agencies will, at the very least, require some sort of legal review for actions over a certain dollar threshold.

DOCUMENTING POSTAWARD ACTIONS AND PROVIDING POSTAWARD NOTIFICATIONS

If you have awarded a competitive contract, the unsuccessful offerors in the competitive range have the right to request a postaward debriefing. A debriefing is intended to let those offerors know why they weren't selected and how they can do better in the future. It is also a great tool for defusing the possibility of a protest. Minutes must be taken of the debriefings, and these minutes become part of your overall negotiation record.

Be careful in these debriefings. Although a debriefing is not considered a negotiation (the negotiation is already completed for that action), some contractors use it to start their intel-gathering activities for future negotiations.

Finally, you may have some postaward notifications to send out. Although not part of the negotiation process per se, the result of your labor is not complete until these are done. You have to, of course, let the winning contractor know it won. You also have to let the losers know they lost. You may have to notify the Small Business Administration or the Department of Labor about the award. Check the FAR and your agency regulations about these postaward notifications.

Manager Alert

Although a debriefing is not considered a negotiation, some contractors use it to start their intel-gathering activities for future negotiations.

PREPARING THE CONTRACT, AWARD, OR AGREEMENT DOCUMENT

You're now ready to create the document that completes the process. Usually this is the contract award document, but it could also be a contract modification.

It could be something else, like how to handle a warranty problem, a blanket purchase agreement, a basic ordering agreement, or a basic agreement. It could be an agreed-to small business subcontracting plan or a delivery order or task order against an existing contract. It could be settling final indirect cost rates or agreeing to a forward rate pricing agreement. It could be settling a dispute or protest or informally agreeing on how to handle contract performance issues. It could be a memorandum of understanding with another federal agency or even an agreement reached with your own program office.

Each of these documents will have its own particular preparation requirements. You'll need to check the FAR and your own agency's policies for guidance on the particulars, which can vary not just by agreement or document type but sometimes by dollar value. Some agencies may require an additional round of approvals after the agreement document has been prepared.

Chapter 39

FINAL THOUGHTS

Some experts say negotiation is an art. Some experts say it is more proper to call the practice of negotiation a skill. They argue that the ability to practice an art is inherent—something you are either born with or not—while the ability to practice a skill can be taught, learned, and improved by practice, even if you are not born with a gift. I believe the effectiveness of practicing any *art* can be improved by acquiring *skills*.

Anyone, whether born with a natural talent to negotiate or not, can improve by acquiring negotiation skills through reading, training, observing, and experience. These skills must be honed by practice and new skills must be constantly acquired to improve results.

It is my hope that this book has exposed you to some tools you can add to your arsenal to improve your negotiation results. You may already know some of them. You may know better ways of applying some of them. Some of them just may not work for you. But if even one proves useful to you in the future, you've gotten worth out of this book that could pay immeasurable benefits later.

My challenge to you is to constantly improve. Continually look for ways to improve, increase, and hone your negotiation skills. Read every book you can. Observe every session you can. Grab a mentor who's a good, seasoned negotiator. Learn from your mistakes—and you'll make some. Better yet, learn from the mistakes of others. Use your everyday negotiation experiences to gain insight into becoming a better government negotiator. Most of all, have fun when you negotiate. Remember, you have little control over what happens to you, but you have all the control in the world over how you *react* to what happens to you. Good luck in all your future negotiations!

Manager Alert
Learn from your mistakes—and you'll make some. Better yet, learn from the mistakes of others.

REFERENCES AND RESOURCES

Here are some excellent, timeless books I believe will be particularly helpful in furthering your study of negotiation. Every serious negotiator should have these books in in his or her library. Happy reading!

Cohen, Herb, *You Can Negotiate Anything* (Bantam Books, 1982).

Dawson, Roger, *Secrets of Power Negotiating* (Career Press, 2010).

Fisher, Roger, William L. Ury, and Bruce Patton, *Getting to Yes: Negotiating Agreement without Giving In* (Penguin Books, 2011).

Hindle, Tim, *Essential Managers: Negotiating Skills* (DK Publishing, Inc., 1998).

McIntyre, LeGette, *Essentials for Government Contract Negotiators* (Management Concepts, 2006).

Shapiro, Ronald M., Mark A. Jankowski, and James Dale, *The Power of Nice* (Wiley & Sons, 2001).

INDEX

A
agenda, 25
allowing other side to make opening statement, 99–100
ambiguous authority tactic, 53–54
anger tactic, 71–72

B
bracketing tactic, 55–56

C
caucus tactic, 49–50
checking availability, 93
clearing schedules, 92–93
climate control tactic, 65–66
closing negotiations
    ambiguous authority, 108–109
    either/or, 109–110
    ensuring total agreement, 110–111
    making everyone feel like winner, 111–112
    methods, 108
    power, 109
    preparation, 107
    silent, 110
    split-the-difference, 110
    total agreement, 108
conducting negotiations, 103–106
coupling tactic, 61–62

D
decoy tactic, 85–86
deliberate mistake tactic, 87–90
deliberate omissions and errors, 90
documenting negotiations
    importance, 113
    post award actions and notifications, 115
    preparing contract, award, or agreement document, 115–116
    price negotiation memorandum, 114
    release of claims, 114
    required reviews and approvals, 115

E
empty pockets tactic, 63–64
establishing authority, 98

F
fait accompli, 81
first tactic, 100
frustration tactic, 77–78

G
gathering data, 7–8
goals
    best value, 2
    importance of, 1
    performance-based contracting, 2–3
good cop/bad cop tactic, 47–48
guilt-trip tactic, 75–76

I
introductions, 97

L
listening, 100–101
lock-in tactic, 81–83
lunch breaks, 95

M
making opening statement, 99

N

nibble tactic, 51–53

O

opening statements, 99–100
order-of-issues tactic, 45–46

P

personal attack tactic, 73–74
phony facts, 87–90
plan
    background information, 17–18
    importance, 17
    major issues, 19
    negotiation objectives, 18–19
    overall objectives, 17
    schedule and logistics, 22–23
    strategy, 19–22
    team members, 18
prenegotiation objectives, 8–10

Q

question tactic, 37–39

R

researching other party
    companies, 11–12
    information gathering tips, 14–15
    information sources, 13–14
    negotiators, 12–13
reserving rooms, 92

roles
    bad cop, 28–29
    good cop, 28
    sweeper, 30
    team leader, 27
    technocrat, 29–30

S

set-aside tactic, 57–58
setting up the room, 93–94
silence tactic, 41–42
strength-in-numbers tactic, 67–68

T

tactics, importance of, 31–32
take it or leave it, 82
team
    briefing, 6
    characteristics, 5
    members, 6
time investment tactic, 35
time pressure tactic, 33–35
tradeoff tactic, 59–60
trial balloon tactic, 39

V

verifying other side's authority, 98
vise tactic, 43

W

walk-in-the-woods tactic, 69–70
walkout tactic, 79–80